D E D I C A T I O N

*This book is dedicated to my brother George Christoforou and
to all others who gave their lives for the liberation of Cyprus.*

CLEANTHIS P. GEORGIADES

Former Gymnasium director, Director of Education, Education adviser

HISTORY OF CYPRUS

New revised Edition in English with 200 photos

SECOND ENGLISH EDITION

PUBLISHER

DEMETRAKIS CHRISTOPHOROU

Michael Karaoli 8A Engomi
(Kykko Area)
Tel. 356150, 361310, Fax 590890

Translation from the Greek
Lonias Efthyvoulou

ISBN: 9963-568-55-6

Colour photographs
by JACK IACOVIDES

Phototypesetting - paging by DOROGRAPHICS LTD, Tel. 445116 Nicosia

Printing by kASSOULIDES - SPANOS LTD, Tel. 482361, Nicosia

PREFACE BY THE REPUBLIC'S PRESIDENT
GLAFCOS CLERIDES

The contribution of Cleanthis Georgiades to the expansion of learned writing on Cyprus, is well known.

He has dedicated a considerable part of his literaturary career to exploration and investigation of sources on Cyprus history. He has also drawn conclusions which are of use to all who are interested in studying the island's progress through history.

His passion for research commenced during his university student years. He took part in a literaturary competition announced by Archbishop Cyril the Third, on the thesis: «The First Inhabitants of Cyprus». His literary work, «The Origin of the Cypriots», was the result

of his research. The Athens Academy, which judged the works submitted, awarded it first prize.

This was the spark of inspiration which led to his continued researches. «The History of Cyprus», was the result. Constantly revised during the past 30 years, this work has been taught in Secondary Schools in Cyprus.

The decision to have this work translated into English, will give the opportunity to foreign visitors to the island, to foreign students, to education establishments, as well as to expatriate Greeks and Greek Cypriots, to learn about our own history.

5

The first President of the Republic of Cyprus, Archbishop Makarios the Third, who died on 3 August 1977, leaving his people without a leader at the most critical milestone of their history.

A FEW WORDS FROM THE PUBLISHER

In fulfilling an old wish of mine, today, I give to the foreign language reader a history of Cyprus, written by our great historian, Cleanthis P. Georgiades. It is augmented and brought up to our own days, enriched with colour photographs. For years now, and with the official approval of the Ministry of Education it has beem taught in our schools.

I have always felt the absence of a history of Cyprus in English. For this reason, I did not take into consideration the great difficulties and cost in order to give to all those who have come to love our so beautiful island, and to all foreign students in our senior and important educational establishments in our country, the opportunity to learn of its history, and our history.

The Publisher
Demetrakis Christoforou

A SHORT GEOGRAPHY OF CYPRUS

Geographic -
Historic
relationship

Although this book is not about geography, a short topographic description of Cyprus becomes essential. It is best to examine historic events after a knowledge of the area in which they have taken place. It is natural that area plays an important role. The location of a country, it's terrain and character are very relevant factors to this country's development and progress, it's march through history.

The position of
Cyprus

Cyprus lies in the North Eastern corner of the Mediterranean Sea. Cyprus is barely 37 miles(60 km) from Asia Minor to the North, 65 miles (105 km) from Syria to the East, and 190 miles (306 km) from Egypt in the South. The Island of Rhodes is also not far away, some 215 miles (346 km) to the North West.

The area of Cyprus

In area Cyprus is the third largest island in the Mediterranean. It is smaller than Sicily and Sardenia, larger than Crete and Corsica. Strabo, the famous geographer, had estimated it's circumnavigation at 3,420 stadia, which is equivalent to 342 miles. Lord Kitchener found the exact same number when he mapped the island with modern equipment, and produced one of the most accurate maps of Cyprus. From the Westernmost Cape Drepanum to the Easternmost Cape of Apostolos Andreas, the island is 140 miles long and 60 miles wide. It has an area of 3,589 square miles.

The shores of
Cyprus

The ancients compared the shape of Cyprus to a Galatean shield, or to the stretched hide of an ox. It's shape provides a great mumber of bays and inlets, which provided safe haven to the mariners who plied the Mediterranean Sea from very ancient times. Bearing in mind the means of travel in antiquity, these bays and havens provide us with an explanation for the close trading relations which the island developed with neighbouring countries. Kourion (Curium), Amathus, Kition (Citium), Salamis, Lapithos and Soloi, they are al mentioned by Strabo as safe havens.

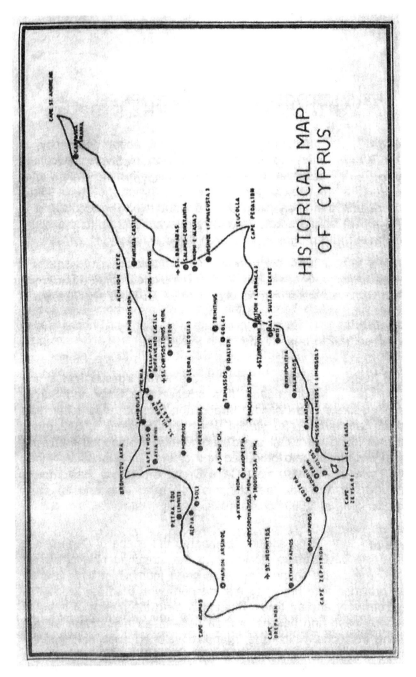

Historical Map of Cyprus

The land -
mountains

Cyprus could be described as a mountainous country. We have two mountain ranges which stretch right across it's entire length. The Troodos is massive and covers most of the island's Western and Southern area. The Pendadaktylos is much narrower and lies along the North shore. The highest peaks are in the Troodos range with Mount Olympus or Chionistra, rising to 6,404 feet. Other high peaks are those of Adelphoi at 5.440 feet, Papoutsa at 5,230, Macheras at 4,650 and Kykko at 4,400. The highest peak in the Pendadaktylos is Kyparissovouno at 3,357 feet, followed by Buffavento at 3,131 and Saint Hilarion at 2,350. The Pendadaktylos peaks, which give the range it's name is only 2,430 feet.

The forests in
antiquity

Both mountain ranges are covered by forests which, however, were much thicker and more extensive in the island's antiquity. It is on record, that in their efforts to create more farm land, the kings of ancient Cyprus allowed their subjects to cut down and destroy the forests for this purpose. These ancient Cyprus forests, however, also provided vast quantities of timber which was exported to Egypt and other countries which needed it to build their fleets. For a very short period in history, these forests also made Cyprus a mistress of the sea. These forests also helped in expansion of the copper and pottery industries by supplying ample fuel for the furnaces. Copper and pottery from Cyprus were exported to all the known countries of antiquity.

The forests
today

Many different varieties of pine, together with plane trees, scrub oak and other trees make up the island's flora. Large areas of forest were destroyed in 1974, during the Turkish invasion of the island, when they were deliberately bombed and set on fire. The rare cedar forest of the island was also badly endangered. Extensive forests like those of Stavros,. Saint Hilarion, Halevka and Kantara suffered greatly. Reforestation in the free areas, since the invasion, has restored much of the damage, but it will take many years before the forests are fully developed once again. In the occupied North, however, the situation remains tragic as the forests of the entire Pendadaktylos range can testify.

Animals
and birds

In antiquity the forests of Cyprus held a great vareity of wild animal and bird life. Boar, wild sheep and goats, such as the mufflon, deer as well as hare and foxes, were the usual game hunted. If we are to judge from scenes depicted on mosaics uncovered by the archaeologists, mainly in Paphos, as well as from artifacts and illustrations, we can be sure that wild cats such as leopard and lion, were also to be found. Partridge and the francoline were also extensively hunted. Today all this wild game has vanished. Partridge and hare are practically the only game left. The mufflon which has survived because of protective measures, is the only large game left. It was near extinction until the Department of Forests started breeding, and then releasing it in the forest areas.

The plains   Cyprus has extensive and very fertile plains between it's mountain ranges. The two plains of the Mesaoria and Morphou are the largest. These two plains which run into each-other made up for good of bad years according to whether there was enough rain or drought. There are smaller plains South of the Troodos and North of the Pendadaktylos, along the shore. Smaller fertile and cultivated valleys are also to be found in the Troodos range, such as the Solea, Marathasa, Pitsillia and Tilliria.

Rivers and   There can be no serious mention of rivers in Cyprus today. In antiquity, and thanks to its lush forests, the island, by all accounts, boasted of large rivers which flowed all the year. Today, however, there are only small and large winter torrents which are fed by rains and snow in the mountains during the winter months. On maps they are described as rivers. In wet years, when there is ample rain and snow, some of these rivers maintain a flow into early summer. This is not very usual because the island is prone to lengthy droughts because of lack of rain. Until recently, water from these rivers just flowed into the sea. Dam construction, which continues under the government's water conservation policy, has guaranteed usable quantities of water, but again this relies on rainfall.

Mineral wealth   By comparison to it's area the island is rich in mineral wealth. Most of the island's ancient mines were still in operation until recently. Cypriot copper mines were known in antiquity and copper was exported to all known countries of that time. Copper was also the reason for the rich expansion of Cypriot civilization which reached high peaks of development. However, copper was also the cause of Cyprus becoming the prey of conquerors throughout its history. At the same time, the island owes its Hellenic background and civilization to this copper.

Cyprus products   Cyprus was known throughout antiquity for the excellence of its produce. Wines and olive oil were among the best known, apart from its minerals. However, wheat and barley, as well as fruit, such as pears and pomegranates were praised by ancient writers such as Pliny and by Atheneos. Perfumes were also manufactured from the island's abundant wild flowers. They were exported in special vials which were found in many of the neighbouring countries and especially in Egypt. Opium, made from wild poppies was also one of the exports to ancient Egypt. The most important exports today are potatoes and citrus fruit as well as market vegetables grapes and wines.

Known names for   The island was known by many different names
Cyprus   in antiquity. The most ancient known name, mentioned in Egyptian texts of the 15th century B.C., was that of Alasia. The same name was also used for the island by the Mycenaean - Achaeans who first settled on the island as merchants and traders in the areas of Engomi, Kition and Kourion. There is one view that the name Alasia was not used for the entire island, but only for one city built by the Mycenaean - Achaeans and was used as their trading center. This city was excavated near the village of Engomi, close to ancient Salamis. There are numerous and conflicting views as to when the island was first known as Cyprus. It is, however, certain that in the ninth century B.C., when the Homeric epics were written, the island was known as Cyprus, and Homer does refer to it under that name. He also refers to the goddess Aphrodite with the adjective «Cypria», Other known and used names for the island were Makaria, Sfikia, Aeria, Menois, and others. These names, however, did not last long, and they were rather used as adjectives in describing the island.

Conclusions   It is clear that because of its position, Cyprus was used as a way - station by any of the powers that wanted contact or trade with Asia Minor, Syria, Palestine, and Egypt. The Eastern and Southern harbours were used for trade with Egypt and Syria and those in the North, obviously for trade with Asia Minor. The two mountain ranges which divide the island into parallel sections, with their defensible mountain passes, contributed to the establishment of separate kingdoms, which often clashed with each other. These clashes were the result of any unequal devision of resources or were due to racial differences. The island's wealth and mineral resources made it the target for attack, conquest or pillage by pirates. The island was thus ravaged or conquered by a succession of masters throughout it's long history.

THE PREHISTORIC ERA

Divisions of prehistory   The prehistoric era of Cyprus spans some five thousand years, from the sixth to the first millenium B.C. Certain man-made items found on Kyrenia and at Kataliondas, prove conclusively that the island was inhabited even before the sixth millennium B.C. at a time which can be described as Mesolithic, or Paleolithtic. These items, however, are so scattered that sofar there can be no mention of a pro-neolithic era on the island. By contrast, the period between the sixth and the first millennium B.C., has become known to us through a large number of settlements which have been either fully excavated, or whose existence has been established by large scale test trenches. We can thus speak with relative certainty about events which took place during this lengthy period and we can also separate it into segments. We can discern three distinct such divisions. The Neolithic, 5,800-3,000 B.C.; the Chalcolithic, 3,000-2,300 B.C.; and the Copper Age, 2,300-1,050 B.C.

A. THE NEOLITHIC PERIOD

Milestones   The Neolithic (literally new stone) era, which is the longest in the island's prehistory, is represented by a considerable number of settlements sited, as a rule, either in valleys or in the foothills, where flowing rivers or springs of water were to be found. Based on the elements characteristic to each one of these settlements, archaeologists have established distinctive milestones or stations within this Neolithic era. They are: The Neolithic IA, 5,800-5,250 B.C., during which the use of stone and bone was the exclusive material for the making of weapons and tools. The Neolithic IB, 5,250-5,000 B.C., during which, and in parallel to the use of stone and bone, we have the use of clay for making home utensils. We then have a dead period of 1,500 years during which it is believed that the island was deserted. We then have The Neolithic II period, 3,500-3,000 B.C. during which clay becomes the nearly exclusive material for making household items.

The Neolithic
IA period

This is the first known stage of neolithic civilization in Cyprus and it is represented by settlements found in diametrically opposite parts of the island and at great distances from each other. Some are found in the center of Southern Cyprus (Chirokitia and Kalavassos-Tenta), another in the South East (Cape Greco), another at the most Easternmost tip (Agios Andreas Kastros), another in the center of Northern Cyprus (Troulli in Kerynia District) and a sixth West of Soloi in North Western Cyprus (Petra tou Limniti). This wide distribution testifies to the extent of habitation in Cyprus and points to the island's importance right from the first years of human habitation on the island. It is considered certain that more systematic excavations, will bring to light more such settlements primarily in the Paphos area where the existence of Neolithic sites has been established at different times.

Chirokitia
settlement

The setlement at Chirokitia is the most significant, because it's size in area, points to the existence of a well-organised community, It is built on a slope near the village with the same name, and is situated near a river. In its hayday it must have been much larger, and it has all the elements of a developed civilization which can in no way be described as primitive. Some fifty structures have sofar been excavated but there are a number of others which have not yet been touched. They are separated into two groups by a high stone wall, which could have been a street leading down to the river, or it could have been a fortification. The foundations of these structures are circular and they are built of native river stone. A wooden support must have existed in the center to help hold up a conical roof. This gave the whole structure the shape of a dome, the walls of which must have been built of mud, with the roof made of tree branches.

Traces of worship
of the dead

Traces of a hearth were found in nearly all these stuctures. Skeletons were also found either under the floor or under the entrance. The dead were buried in the crouching position and many of them also had a heavy stone placed on their chest. This indicates that the stone was put there because of a fear that the dead might get up once again. Various weapons and some artifacts, tools and broken cups, were also found by the side of the dead. This, once again, may indicate that the people did believe in some form of life after death, and they thus gave the dead some form of help in these items, for their daily use. In this way they did express some form of worship of the dead.

View of the Chirokitia settlement, the most ancient settlement (5,800-5,250 B.C.) which was discovered in Cyprus. The largest circular structure can be seen after the first hut. It could have been the home of the chief, or a temple. This shows that we are viewing a well structured community.

Life in the settlement	Various items, tools and artifacts, found in these structures, indicate that they were used both as a home, as well as a workshop. The spindle whorls, awls and needles made of bone, indicate that these people had already tamed sheep and goats. It is also certain from other evidence found, that they had tamed oxen as well as pigs. They used wool from the animals to weave clothes. Hand mills and pestles as well as sickle blades show that they also knew about the cultivation of cereals which they obviously ground in order to make bread. Arrowheads and horns from wild sheep and deer show us that these people also hunted game, which must have been abundant in the surrounding forested areas. Vessels of hard stone - andestite - which were made deeper by rubbing them on another, harder stone, and then polished or decorated with relief or etched, testify to the existence not only of a controlled diet but also of an aesthetic desire of these people which is illustrated by these well - made household items. Blades of obsidian, which is not native to Cyprus, but is found in abundance in Asia Minor, and with which they scraped hides, indicate to us that these people had managed to cross the sea to reach the opposite shore and establish contact with other peoples. This communication and contact could also have taken place with other sea-shore settlements of the island such as that of Cape Greco and Agios Andreas-Kastros, where obsidian blades were also found.

Community organisation	All this evidence demonstrates that at Chirokitia we have a well organised society which was very exceptional for that time. The men and women within this society were involved in different organised activities in agriculture, animal husbandry and in hunting. We observe a reverence towards the dead ones an artistic desire and even religiousness. Certain small idols made of andesite depict, very crudely and simply, but in a natural way the form of man or of animals. Perhaps these are a first attempt to give form and shape to a supernatural being which will be worshipped in a more specific manner much later in time. The discovery of one structure with dimensions nearly double those of the rest, is interpreted as being the residence of a chief. This goes to strengthen the belief that the Chirokitia settlement was a well organized and developed community, whose civilization is not representative of the civilization of other primitive inhabitants of the island.

Life in the other settlements of the Neolithic IA period	With the exception of the Petra tou Limniti settlement, where the site does not allow the development of an organised community (tiny islet), but where, in truth, some family of fishermen seems to have sought protection from wild animals, all other settlements of the same period, demonstrate a life style similar to that of the Chirokitia settlement. We find the very same circular structures, nearly similar weapons and tools, similar household items and evidence of the same activities, but with the addition of fishing. In the case of the people of Agios Andreas-Kastros, fishing appears to have been the main activity as evidenced by the amounts of fish bones and shells and their fragments found inside the structures. It is certain that shells, after the contents were consumed, must have been used by the women as a decoration and for making necklaces. Such necklaces were also made of pebbles, thus indicating a clear artistic bent.

First people - were they from Asia Minor or Thessalians? It cannot be established with any degree of certainty, where these first inhabitants of the island came from. The small distance which separates Troulli in the North from Asia Minor, or Agios Andreas-Kastros from Cilicia and Chirokitia from Syria, could perhaps justify the view that Cyprus did receive its first inhabitants from these areas. However, there are fundamental differences between the civilizations of these countries and the Neolithic IA civilization of Cyprus. The many differences between anthropologic remains are even more basic. Based on these remains, and following the study of skulls, some people argue that racially, the first Cypriots are closer to the Balkan people and especially to the Thessalians. These Thessalians, who were on their way to Macedonia and Thrace did pass through Asia Minor and Cilicia to Cyprus. They could also have come to Cyprus from other islands, by crossing the Aegean sea. The civilization which thrived in Thessaly over the same period as the Neolithic IA in Cyprus, supports this theory.

Neolithic IB period Recent archaeological excavations have brought to light three settlements of this period at Denia (Dhenia), Filia (Philia), and Agios Epiktitos in the Kerynia district. Denia (Dhenia) and Filia are in the Morphou area and the main characteristic of these settlements is the clay pottery which appears for the first time in such Neolithic settlements. The shapes are rather simple, bowls and ewers and bottle-shaped jugs. They are usually decorated with concentric circles. They often have wavy lines and other designs which demonstrate an artistic bent which is unusual for that time.

New colonists The use of clay as well as the abandonment of the round structure - At Agios Epiktitos the structures are square with stone walls which in some cases are four meters high - lead us to believe that new colonists must have arrived in Cyprus in the latter part of the sixth millennium B.C. It is believed that they came from Cilicia and that they occupied a large part of Northern Cyprus. If we judge on the basis of a defence structure found at Filia, we can reach the conclusion that the capture of these lands by the new colonists must have been a not so peaceful one. The first vaulted grave was also discovered at Filia. The fact that this grave was independent from the homes, also points to a change in burial customs. During this period, as in subsquent ones, agriculture appears to have been the main activity of these people. Animal husbandry and hunting was the work of the men while women were busy with carding wool, weaving and the grinding of cereals for bread. Women, of course, were also responsible for cooking. The manufacture of pots from clay was also added to these activities of the women, who also decorated them. The tradition prevails in certain areas to this day.

The dead period We have already mentioned the dead period of some 1,500 years between the Neolithic I and Neolithic II periods. We have no evidence on this period as no settlements from this period have been found. The view that the island was deserted by its people cannot be substantiated by any evidence. The most likely is that the people moved to richer areas or safer areas, which have not yet been discovered or which were destroyed without leaving any trace behind them. Only time and more systematic excavation may perhaps shed light upon this period.

The Neolithic II period The period covers some 500 years and is represented by three settlements on the Southern part of the island - - the third layer at Chilokitia, at Kalavassos and Sotira. The type and method of house building is very different and the clay pottery mainly differs in its decoration. Instead of being simply painted as at Filia, and Agios Epiktitos, it is now combed. The term means that before the slip applied on the vase dried, the pot was combed by a toothed tool (Kteni) thus producing light coloured wavy or straight lines. Another basic difference during this period, was in the establishment of special burial grounds for the dead (cemeteries) which indicate a change of view about the dead.

We can see the artistic taste of the ancient Cypriots in their attempts to depict the human form. Even in their primitiveness they suprise the student and researcher of art objects of that distant era. Pictured is a human head made of andesite. (Chirokitia 5,800-5,250 B.C.)

Here we have a whole human figure with very clear facial features, a long neck, and a four-sided body gauged out at the end to indicate legs. (Chirokitia, 5,800-5,250 B.C.)

Colonists from
Palestine
All these basic differences indicate that new colonists were arriving in Cyprus towards the end of the fourth millennium B.C., from different areas, but mostly from Palestine. In parallel periods of time, the civilization of Palestine shows basic similarities to that of Cyprus during the Neolithic II period, at least as it is represented at Kalavassos and Sotira. It is certain that the arrival of new colonists is related to the discovery of copper, which led to large scale migrations of people who sought the new metal wherever they could find it. Cyprus was the country which promised rich deposits of copper.

THE CHALCOLITHIC PERIOD

Cyprus is thickly
inhabited
Some 100 sites have been identified by the archaeologists, who believe they were settled during the Chalcolithic (literally «copper - stone») period which lasted for seven centuries, 3,000 - 2,300 B.C. They are scattered in the North West and Central Cyprus, as well as in forested areas. Only a very small number of them have been excavated. It is believed that this sudden population explosion in Cyprus, and the parallel establishment of such large numbers of settlements is connected to the great movement of people in the East Mediterranean area, the Balkans, and the Near East, driven by the search for copper.

Characteristics of
the period
The characteristics of this period, which is better known through the settlements at Kalavassos B, and at Erimi, as well as the cemetery at Souskiou, near Palaepaphos , is the progress in pottery techiques and in pottery decoration, showing a larger variety of shapes and very careful work in colour decoration, inspired from the plant world as well as simple geometric designs. There is also a return to the circular structure and a division of the residence into two or more apartments. There is also a more intense religious awareness as demonstrated in the manufacture of steatite as well as clay idols which are believed to represent the goddess of fertility. These idols were placed in graves together with other rich offerings of pottery, jewellery and other valuables.

The idols
The idols of this period are particularly characteristic. They are cross-shaped and are carved out of grey of green steatite with surprising mastery. Most of them represent human beings - as a rule women - but often also depict animals. Such

SUMMARY OF THE NEOLITHIC AND
CHALCOLITHIC PERIODS

The first known Cyprus civilisation is traced to the beginning of the sixth millennium B.C. It is represented in settlements of organised communities. This justifies the supposistion that the island was inhabited even before the sixht millennium, but we still do not have sufficient facts to confirm this.

These inhabitants are either descendants of nomads of a time prior to the sixth millennium, or arrivals from Asia Minor and, or Syria and Palestine, or even from Thessaly via Macedonia - Asia Minor- Cilicia - were in a stage of advanced civilisation. They had tamed sheep, goats and cattle. They made clothes from fleece, using tools made of animals bones. They cultivated the earth with cereals and made bread. They also cooked in stone vessels which they deepened and polished in an admirable fashion. They did hunt with stone slings for wild sheep and deer which abounded in the deep forests. Those who lived near the sea, also fished.

Right from the start of their presence on the island, they demonstrate obvious trends of artistic desire and of religious feelings. They decorate both stone, and clay pottery with etched or relief desings to start with and later with brushed or combed patterns. Religous feeling starts with respect of the dead and goes on to near worship. The dead are first buried inside the dwelling, or near the door. Later, burial is in bee-hive tombs in special burial grounds with an abundance of votive offerings, At a later stage, religious feeling is demonstrated in the making of small idols of steatite. The technique is surprising for that time. It is believed they depict some god or goddess - the goddess of fertitily - and the idols are placed in graves, together with other votive offerings, to protect the dead.

A great number of population upheavals took place during the three and a half thousand years of the Neolithic, and Chalcolithic eras. The most important was the arrival of new colonists from Asia-Minor, Syria and Palestine - and perhaps from the Aegean islands of the Cyclades and Rhodes - towards the end of the fourth millennium. They estabilished a great number of settlements moslty in areas where they hoped to find copper. It is certain that by the beginning of the third millennium B.C., they had already discovered cooper bearing strata on a smal scale. This led to even more colonists who settled on the planes of the Mesaoria and the Karpass which, until this time, had been sparcely inhabited. This is turn, inaugurated the third era of Cyprus prehistory, the Copper Era.

Artistic taste at the Chirokitia settlement is not absent. With all the difficulties of working the andesite, the very ancient Cypriot managed to make extremely delicate and beautiful vessels which he smoothed and polished with great patience, like the one in the photograph. (5,800-5,250 B.C.)

And here we have something more. He decorated his vessels in a linear and pointilist style, like the one seen here. It makes one wonder if it is truly the work of people whose only tools were the stone and bones from animals.

In time the Cypriot craftsman gains more experience, and he starts working in harder and more colourful stones. He works with steatite, from which he carves little idols which he places as votive offerings in the graves of his dead. We have an example here of an idol in the shape of a cross. Around its neck it wears a similar cross-shaped miniature idol in relief. (Paphos, 3,000-2,500 B.C.)

A second idol from Souskiou in Paphos carved out of green-grey steatite. The elongated neck is also characteristic here. It is also decorated with an etched design. Chalcolithic era (3,000 - 2,500 B.C.)

We come up against the first clay pots in the settlements of the Neolithic IB era (5,250-5,000 B.C.) also known as protoceramic. The use of clay permits creation of pots with a more delicate shape. We see here a large pithos, with a white surface bearing a linear design of red paint. (Erimi, Chalcolithic era 3,000-2,500 B.C.)

Another pot with a white slip and red paint for its decoration from the Chalcolithic settlement of Erimi. Here we have a pitcher with a pointed base. (3,000-2,500 B.C.)

idols were found at Erimi, but greater numbers came from the cemetery at Souskiou, and this underlines their religious significance.

THE COPPER ERA

Cyprus a true copper lode   The long search for copper which went on through the Chalcolithic era, in the end produced results. Success was so great that Cyprus became a true copper lode and this great abundance of copper had a decisive effect on the island's civilization and historic development, because of the great number of important effects it brought with it.

Wealth, riches Civilization advances   The first effect was the wealth and prosperity it brought to the people. This brought on a truly monumental civilization development. One only has to study the fantastic variety and artistry of the period's pottery from Vouno near Bella Pais, especially its complex and varied decoration. The weapons and tools were made of copper, silver, gold and ivory; the Cypro-Mycenaean pottery from Agios Iakovos, Idalion, Episkopi, Kition and Old Paphos, as well as pottery from other setlements, the architecture and layout of towns and cities such as Engomi and Kition, the sacred architecture, writing and burial customs all of them speak for a tremendous advance of civilization. In one word one has only to study everything that goes to make up a great civilization in order to comprehend the heights which this civilization in Cyprus reached in the 1,250 years of its existence.

Commerce, marine and cultural interaction   The second effect was the expansion of commerce and relations with neighbouring countries. This brought about developments in building of merchant ships, and with it the study and development of maritime navigation. Indirectly, this led to contacts with other civilizations and in the exchange of material and other benefits. In this manner Cyprus developed a maritime tradition which, according to records, led it to become a mistress of the seas, even though this came much later and for only some 30 years, 742-709 B.C. The island imported goods and materials not available in Cyprus both in the form of raw material as well as manufactured items. One of these was faience from which they manufactured exquisite pottery. Alabaster was another, together with gold, ivory and even ostrich eggs which were often found in Cypriot graves. Such ties were developed by Cyprus with Asia Minor, Syria, Palestine, Egypt,

Crete, and the Aegean Islands. Later they were developed with Mycenae itself, and with continental Greece. Apart from copper Cyprus also exported pottery in large quantities. We thus find large quantities of Cypriot pottery in neighbouring countries. It also exported timber, perfumes and opium. Cyprus perfume and opium vials were found in great numbers in graves at Tel-el-Amarna in Egypt.

Domestic Upheaval as a result The third effect came with the readjustment of population within the island itself. The abundance of great weath also caused jealousies and made people move from the poor to the wealthier areas. It was also natural that new settlements were established in the fertile plains of the Mesaoria and the Karpass peninsula. During the second millennium these plains were virtually uninhabited but with time they became not only more populous but also came to claim a great role in the island's history. Some of the important trading centers on the plains were at Kalopsida, Milia, Engomi, Sinda and Agios Iakovos in Eastern Cyprus and at Kition and Kourion (Curium) in the South.

Foreign interference The most significant effect, however, was in the fact that due to its prosperity, Cyprus became the target for foreign intervention and interference by the strong powers in the area. Such interference often took the form of piracy raids, at other times the form of colonization and at other times conquest and foreign domination. We have such an example in the case of Egypt when Pharaoh Thotmes the third in 1470 B.C. imposed a tax on the island. In letters found at Tel-el-Amarna, we are informed that the king of Alasia dispatched presents to Pharaoh Echnaton (Akhenaten), an act denoting that Cyprus was still paying tribute to Egypt at the time the last Pharaoh was in power (1350 - 1340 B.C.).

Castles and Tombs The result of all this foreing interference, as well as the domestic strife, was that great defence works had to be built to protect the cities. Examples of such defence works abound, such as the castle of Nitovikla in the Karpass, another such castle near Agios Sozomenos and the defence post at Krini. Engomi was surrounded by Cyclopean walls and Kition and Idalion were protected by very storng defenses. The discovery of large quantities of arms and the mound at Palaeskoutela which covers a mass grave, are indicative of the disturbed times that shook the island during the copper era.

Colonization   Intervention, in its broader sence, came with colonization, because it was this colonization which defined the ethnic compositon of Cyprus. Such colonization drives came mainly from Asia Minor, whose people were pressured by the Hittites and were forced to move to Cyprus in great numbers, and lastly the Mycenaeans whose power in the Aegean and generally in the East Mediterranean, was continually increasing from the 15th century B.C.

THE MYCENAEANS - ACHAEANS IN CYPRUS

Cyprus - Greece before the 15th century B.C.   Until the 15th century B.C., relations between Greece and Cyprus were very limited. Crete, however, was the exception. Cyprus had commercial relations with Crete, rather sparse at the start of the second millennium B.C., but very frequent from the 17th century B.C., as evidenced by the Minoan pottery found at Morphou and at Agia Irini. This state of affairs did change after the 15th century B.C.

Achaean expansion   By the 15th century B.C., the Acheans became very strong. They had moved into the Peloponnese where they had established strong kingdoms such as Mycenae, Argos, Tiryns, and Pylos. They broke up the Minoan trading centers established there, they adopted elements of the Minoan civilization and established their own Mycenaean civilization. Taking advantage of the defeat of the Hyksos - - who ravaged the East Mediterranean - - by Pharaoh Thotmes the third, they moved East establishing control of trade for themselves. Their first act was to settle their own merchants in trading centers in Crete, Rhodes, Cyprus and Asia Minor, then Syria, Palestine and Egypt. In their trading centers, the emporia, they conducted business side by side with the native traders, thus avoiding local reaction. They won the locals over as allies and thus managed to neutralise the increasing strength of the Hittites. In Cyprus they had such trading centers at Engomi, Kition, Kourion, Old Paphos, Morphou, Agia Irini. They also had such centers in Syria and in Egypt.

Achaeans Hittites   A dynamic people, the Hittites conquered all of Asia Minor and they could not stand the fact that the Mycenaeans had cornered all the trade for themselves. Thus they often clashed and Cyprus felt the after-effects. The Hittites often raided the island and some historians claim that Cyprus came under the Hittite sovereignty. Hittite texts found in their Cappadocean capital indicate that Cyprus was freed of this sovereignty in 1225 B.C. by the king of the Achaeans Attarisijus, who is identified by many as Attreus.

Achaean
sovereignty

Under the Mycenaean sovereignty Cyprus was gradually Hellenised. It is this that Homer stressed when he referred to the king of Paphos Kinyras who presented Agamemnon with a magnificent breast plate made out of copper, gold, pewter and lazurite, for his campaign against Troy. It is certain that Kinyras, who was also a high priest for Aphrodite, was not an Achaean and the fact that he felt the need to make a valuable gift to the chief of the Achaeans, strongly indicates to their sovereignty over the island. The same is also indicated in another reference by Homer to another king, Dmetor Iasides who most certainly was an Achaean king, but the poet does not refer to him as the king of any specific city, but as the king who firmly ruled over the entire island.

Hellenization of
Cyprus

The Trojan war is referred to as the last Achaean large scale campaign. They were forced to seek new colonies as a result of the descent of the Dorians who had started moving South in Greece much earlier than their traditional settlement of the Peloponnesos in 1104 B.C. The Achaeans proceed to establish their colonies in Asia Minor where the Hittite influence started to wane. They also moved into Rhodes and into Cyprus. In Cyprus they were referred to as the heroes of the Trojan war. We have Tefkros (Teucer) who established Salamis. Kifeas (Kepheus) who established Kerynia, Praxandros who established Lapithos, Demophon who founded Aipia, Faliros and Akamas founded Soloi, Agapinor of Paphos, Golgos of Golgoi, the present day Athienou, Chytros of Chytroi and many others, who established colonies at Kourion, Asine and others. According to Achaean custom, each one of these colonies was a kingdom. Thus by the end of the prehistoric era we find Cyprus totally Hellenised.

The Cypriot
script

The most ancient Cypriot inscriptions were found at Engomi, and they were written in an unknown language as yet undeciphered. They date back to the 16th cenrury B.C. and the script is similar to one found in Crete and in Mycenaean Greece at Tiryns, Thebes, at Myceanae itself and at Pylos. Some 566 such tablets were found in the palace of Nestor at Pylos. Efforts to decipher the script continue. It is believed that the script arrived in Cyprus through the Cretan merchants and that it was mainly used to keep accounts.

A unique example of it´s kind. It is a model of a fenced open air sanctuary at the time of worship, from the necropolis of Vounos. The "initiated" are offering a sacrifice to three deities with a human body and the face of a bull, with snakes hanging from their arms. We know that the bull symbolised the god of fertility, and the snake symbolised the nether god of death. Worship in this sanctuary, therefore, is of these two gods. The chief priest with a crown on his head is sitting on a throne ready for the sacrifice of oxen, which we can see penned in one corner of the sanctuary. Some initiates are attending the rites inside the fenced area. However, a non-initiated curious character is trying to peek in and see what is going on by scaling the wall from the outside, near the main gate. (2,100-2,000 B.C.)

Cypriot religion until arrival of the Mycenaeans   Cypriots of the Neolithic era did have some undeveloped religious sentiments mainly expressed through burial customs, in votive offerings to dead, and perhaps in some form of sacrifice. As the centuries went by, this religious sentiment became strong and was expressed through depiction of some supreme being, represented on small idols and then it rose to high levels of expression during the copper era, when sacred places for worship were designed and built. Divinity now took some more specific meaning. It is personified in the goddess of fertility and the terrestrial death god. The goddess does not have one specified image but is worshipped sometimes in the form of a woman, often holding her breasts, or a child in her arms. At other times she is worshipped in the form of a bull whose head is depicted etched or carved on pottery, rings, etc., and at other times in the form of a horned god or a god often standing on a talent of copper, to indicate his importance as the god protector of mines, the source of wealth and income for the people. The terrestrial death god was always worshiped in the form of a snake.

Images of sacred places   An enclosed circular courtyard, with the images of divinity at one end, was the original sacred place where the gods were worshipped. We find this depicted in items of unique value found at Vounos, Kotsiatis and Kalopsida. They depict a sacred place, and these items were placed in graves as votive offerings to invoke divine protection. The one from Vounos is of great importance. It depicts in detail a priest ready to sacrifice oxen in honour of three totem-pole - like figures with the heads of bulls, holding snakes in their arms. Some «initiated» people are also shown attending the rites. A certain inquisitive person is depicted hanging on the wall which he has scaled from the outside of the enclosure in order to secretly watch the ceremomy. This detail, alone, indicates it's mystic character.

Minoan and Mycenaean influence on religion   Close commercial ties between Cyprus and Minoan Crete, as well as with the rest of the Aegean world, during the second quarter of the second millennium B.C., also had an influence on Cypriot religion as well as worship itself. Sacred trees, animals, and birds, the horns of consecration, the double axe, the sacred pillar, the table of offerings, all these had a direct influence and gained a special significance in Cypriot religion and worship in the very same way they had in Minoan and Aegean religion and worship. The sacred places of worship were no more the enclosed courtyards. They became temples like the ones at Agios Iacovos, Agia Irini, and later, more specifically, at

Engomi, Kition and Palaepaphos, where the temples brought to light are purely Mycenaean.

Hellenism in religion and worship It is certain that the Mycenaeans, both as merchants, from the 15th to the 12th centuries B.C., as well as the last permanent colonists of the island from the 12th century B.C., did bring to the island their own gods which they worshiped. We do know who these gods were from the inscriptions at Pylos and Knossos. They were Zeus and Hera, Athena and Artemis, as well as Apollo. They could also have been Poseidon, Demeter, and Dionysus in company with Hermes and Ares. By the start of the historic era, all these gods were fully established and this points to the Hellenization of Cypriot religion and worship. Some of the kingdoms had their own protector god, worshipped with special pomps and rites.

The worship of Aphrodite Despite the Hellenization of the island, the worship of the goddess of fertility could not be completely uprooted from the island. She thus evolved into the goddess Aphrodite, the protectress not of one single kingdom on the island, but of the entire island itself. The myth of her birth off Paphos underlines the fact. The Hellenes of that historic era admitted Aphrodite as a pre-Hellenic goddess and her adjective «Cypria» mentioned in Homer as «Kypris» underlines her pancyprian character. Idols depicting men with cymbals, musicians and dancers can only commemorate the festivals held at Palaepaphos in her honour. Ceremonies honouring Aphrodite - Astarte were held at Kition while in Amathus we have them commemorating Aphrodite and Adonis.

Here, instead of a whole sanctuary, we have one faithful offering a libation in a ceremonial vessel, before three deities in the form of bulls heads. (Kalopsidha, 2,100-2,000 B.C.)

Here we have one of the finest examples of votive ceremonial vessels with plastically rendered images on its rim, from Vounos. The images consist of three types of animals and three bowls. The body of the vessel is decorated with an incised linear design. (2,100-2,000 B.C.)

A very valuable find from Vounos. On a five-legged table we have human-shaped figures leading two pairs of oxen drawing a plough of the same kind that the Cypriot farmer used only a few years ago. Two other figures are holding a trough with the seed in it, ready for sowing by the farmers. (2,100-2,000 B.C.)

Human figures before troughs, infants in cradles, women and animals, a whole agricultural scene, plastically rendered, some figures as if in high velief along the entire rim of this exquisite vessel. (Margi 2,000-1,850 B.C.)

34

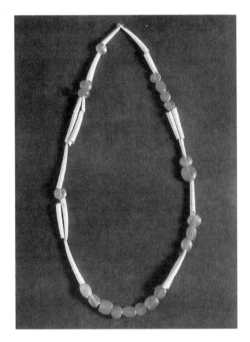

The coquettishness and love of style of Neolithic women is seen here. We have a necklace of dentalia shells and elongated and round beads of cornaline. It was found in the last chronological stratum of Chirokitia. (3,500-3,000 B.C.)

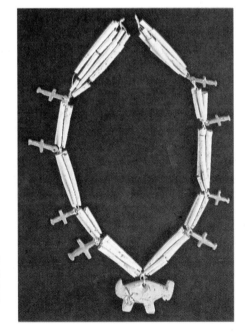

Another Chalcolithic necklace (3,000-2,500 B.C.). Ornaments between the dentalia are impressive. They depict the cross-shaped small idols, with the exception of the one at the bottom which is animal-shaped.

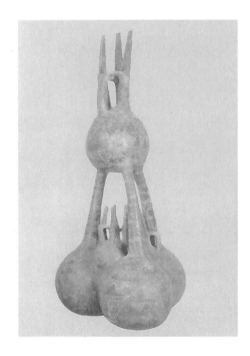

Examples of the imagination of the craftsman at Vounos settlement are to be found in the simple or the composite vases of clay with relief, incised or plastically rendered decoration. Here we see a composite vase of unusual shape and technique. (2,100-2,000 B.C.)

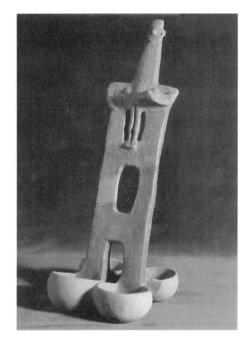

Another unusual vessel with four bowls, the common handle of which is made up of a plank-like idol of a woman holding an infant in her arms. (2,100-2,000 B.C.)

We have an unusually large number of plank-shaped idols, found in the graves of Copper-age. In these idols the deity takes a human form and is placed in the grave to protect the dead. In this photograph the idol has two heads. The linear incised decoration, with the lines filled with a white substance, gives the red polished surface an exceptional artistic appearance. (Denia 2,000 B.C.)

This plank-shaped idol is very simple with the head and neck joined together. It is in the same technique as the one above. (Vounos 2,000 B.C.)

A large pitcher with two parallel necks, one of which is decorated with two human figures in relief, and the other with a horned animal. The body of the pitcher is decorated with bands in relief. (Vounos 2,100-1,850 B.C.)

An extremely beautiful and deep jar of red polished clay with its upper part and its interior black. The rim is decorated with four projections two of which end in simple and single animal heads, and the other two in double such heads. The incised decoration again filled with a white substance, is very rich and varied. (2,100-2,000 B.C.)

A large red-polished pitcher from Lapithos of the early copper age. The upper part of the handle is decorated with a miniature pitcher and opposite it a table of offerings with two female figures, a jug and a cup at the end. The base of the handle is decorated with a dove having cups on either side of it of the same type as that on the table. (2,000-1,850 B.C.)

An item discovered at Vounos with an extremely important value in the study of worship. It is an offering table with a jug in the centre and two cups, one each on the ends. (2,100-2,000 B.C.)

A large rare form of a pot from Kochatis. In an astonishing manner the craftsman depicts two birds swallowing water which they drink from a cup between them. (2,000 - 1,850 B.C.)

A very beautiful pitcher with a globular body, three cylindrical necks and a spout opposite the handle.

A globular pitcher with a long and upright cylindrical neck with a handle rising from the pots shoulder and half-way up the neck. Two moulded deer on either side of the neck give a special charm to the pot with their branched antlers. It is to be seen in the Pierides Foundation Museum in Larnaca. (2,000-1,850 B.C.)

This hemispherical vessel also comes from Vounos. Two birds are perched on two cylindrical bases along its rim.They look like doves, and each has a cup in front of it. (2,000-1,850 B.C.)

41

A composite ritualistic red polished vase of the early copper age from Polemidhia. Three cups resting on elongated stems springing up from a common base, are joined by horizontal supports.

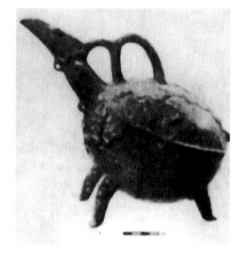

An animal-like vessel from Paramali. It´s egg-shaped body is supported on four legs which are slightly curved. It bears snakes in relief on its body. (2,000-1,850 B.C.)

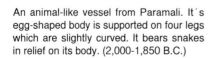

42

We have a very great number of animal-shaped vessels found in graves from the early copper age and later. It is not known what the craftsman wanted to depict with the vessel in this picture. His imagination, however, can be seen both in the shape, as well as in its decoration. (2,000-1,850 B.C)

The craftsman is much more specific in this example. He has formed a saddled donkey - with the saddle similar to those used today. It looks as if it will bray any minute. (2,000-1,850 B.C.)

White vessels with a red linear decoration are another type which is characteristic of the last phase of the early copper age. Here we have a boat-shaped vessel. Two riders are back at each end. (Vounos 2,000-1,850 B.C.)

An animal-shaped vessel depicting a bull from Soloi. The short legs and stub of a tail, by contrast to the long horns and large nose give the vessel a comical character. (2,000-1,850 B.C.)

44

An unusual painted vessel of the middle copper age (1,850-1,600 B.C.), from Agia Paraskevi. It has a white surface bearing linear decoration in dark colour. The string-hole projections in pairs on its neck and sides, give it a special charm. This is enhanced by the decoration all over its surface.

A very beautiful Mycenaean vase of the three handled amphora type and an unusual and loud decoration on its shoulder. It was found with hundreds of others in an Angastina grave. 14th century B.C.

White slip vessels are the customary technique of pot-making in the late copper age. The above is a hemispherical bowl with a wishbone handle, and a rounded base. It was found at Kythrea. The painted motifs separate the surface into panels.

A tankard of the same type and style has a ring base. The decoration consists of latticed lozenges and elongated dots in vertical and horizontal rows, separating the surface into small panels.

A view of the defensive wall of Engomi. The public buildings, the sanctuaries, the copper-smith workshops, the rich finds of mainly Mycenaean style, make Engomi one of the most important centers of prehistoric civilization in Cyprus. The town planning of the city was perfect for that epoch.

Wine vessels with ringed base are the most representative examples of Cypriot shape, making in the latter copper era. The entire construction shape, thin walls, relief decoration demonstrate that they are imitations of copper pots. On the left such a jug with a single neck and above, one with twin necks, of the 14th to the 13th century B.C.

The famous "crater of Zeus." Zeus is the centre theme of the decoration . He holds the Homeric scales of destiny and judges the fate of the warriors. They are seated in the chariot before him. It is a literal depiction of the Homeric verses from the Iliad (A29ff). The presence of a bird (an omen) the wings of which indicate that it is flying on the right of the warriors shows that the scales tip in their favour. Referrence to the bird flying on the right hand side as a good omen is mentioned by Homer in the Odyssey (Ω292ff).

Another Mycenaean crater with a mythological representation. On each one of its two sides it depicts two warriors in a chariot who, in terror, flee from a gigantic bird. This brings to mind the chase and the capture of the fearsome bird Zu of Eastern mythological origins. A crater decorated with the same theme was found at Ugarit, where, it is believed, the inhabitants of Engomi maintained a trading post.

The marine world was a beloved decorative motif, specially on Mycenaean pottery. Two huge octopi decorate this amphoroid crater, the entire surface of which is covered by their tentacles. Early 14th century B.C.

The largest of a number of clay tablets found at Engomi with the Cypro-Minoan script, which, unfortunately, and despite efforts by learned language experts, still remains undeciphered. It is believed that the text is of poetry verses. 13th century B.C.

A beautiful amphora-like crater of the 13th century B.C. Two bulls, facing each other, have between them a stylized sacred tree which was a basic element of Mycenaean religion.

A very beautiful bowl dating to the 14th century B.C. from a grave in Engomi. The exterior surface bears inlaid decoration in gold and a black substance. It consists of six bull heads with lotus flowers between them and rosettes at the bottom.

A golden elliptical pectoral from Engomi. Two sphinxes, facing each other, have a stylized tree between them. 13th century B.C.

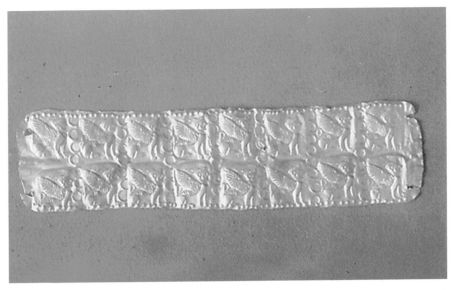

A second golden diadem from Engomi. It consists of two rows of four-sided frames, in each of which there is an embossed seated winged Sphinx of Mycenaean technique, 13th century B.C.

A copper, gold-plated ring from Engomi. On its setting it depicts a lion incised in an exquisite natural manner. The movement of the animal, the lithe curve of the body, and its turned head, illustrate an object of high quality Mycenaean art. 13th century B.C.

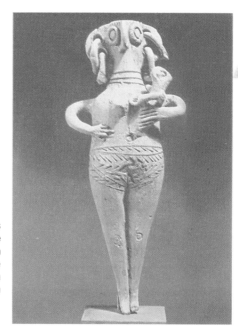

Eastern influence on this type of small idol is evident. They are met throughout the Mycenaean world and are abundant in Cyprus. They are identified as idols of the godess Astarte. It shows a naked woman with the head and face of a bird, holding an infant in her arms. 14th century B.C.

A golden necklace of the 13th century B.C., from Engomi. It is made up of 10 beads in the shape of an 8-shaped shield, connected with triple golden tubes.

This golden necklace comes from Agios Iakovos and is made up of seven beads in the shape of a pomegranate and eight in the shape of a date. In the center it has a talisman of Haematite incised with a cuneiform inscription. 14th century B.C.

Earrings are the most usual items to be found in graves as votive offerings. They are of copper or of gold. Here we have golden ones in the shape of a bull´s head. A similar pair is found at Kouklia. 13th century B.C.

A mirror handle of exquisite workmanship made of ivory. It was found at Kouklia. On the upper part of the handle, and on both its sides there is an illustration of the labour of Hercules in which he slew the lion of Nemea. The rest of the handle is also beautifully carved with leaves and linear pattern in relief. 13th century B.C.

A golden and enamelled royal scepter from Kourion. There are two vultures perched on an orb in the upper portion, of high artistic quality. Its presence is very important as it proves the existence of "scepter-bearing" kings from the 12th century B.C.

A copper statue of the 12th century B.C. depicting the well known "horned" Apollo, from Engomi. The youthful god with delicate features wears a conical hat with two horns. Remnants of sacrifice were found at the spot where it was discovered, together with masks in the shape of bulls' heads. Priests who performed the sacrifices covered their faces with these masks.

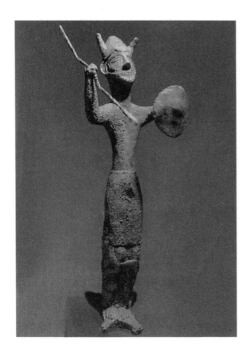

A copper statuette of a bearded god standing on an ingot of copper in order to underline his identity as a protector of mines. He wears a conical hat with bull´s horns, just like the "horned" Apollo. He wears shinguards and is armed with a sword and a shield. Just like in the case of the "horned' Apollo, sacrificial remnants were also found at the spot where it was found. 12th century B.C.

The use of masks is related to religion from very ancient times. This relationship is seen more clearly during the historic era through the use of masks by the actors in a drama. We know that the origins of this lie in Dionysian rites. This is a well-preserved mask from Dali, and is now in the Louvre Museum. 12th century B.C.

There are two thousand terracotta statues and small idols which the Swedish Archaelogical Expedition discovered in 1929 in the sanctuary of Agia Irene, just as they had been positioned around an altar. Priests bearing bulls' masks of their faces, sphinxes, centaurs, bulls, chariots, all of them contributing to the creation of an invaluable treasure. Seventh to sixth century B.C. It is exhibited in the Cyprus Museum in Nicosia.

THE HISTORIC ERA

The first
centuries
The start of the historic era is usually placed in the 11th century B.C., at the time when the Iron Age starts. It is clear that the first centuries are rather dim as we do not have written records of that time, to furnish us with direct information on historical facts. Knowledge, therefore, comes from indirect sources which are such, that they do not allow us to study the island's history with any degree of certainty.

The Phoenicians
There were no out of the ordinary developments in Cyprus between the 11th and 9th centuries B.C. The Achaeans, who had abandoned Peloponnisos had to strengthen the colonies which they had established and busied themselves with organizing their various kingdoms. Being busy with this, they neglected all efforts towards reorganising their naval strength. In this they furnished an opportunity to a new and active people, the Phoenicians, to capture commercial activity which they expanded to the Pillars of Hercules - - to Gibraltar. Tyre and Sidon were turned into the largest commercial centers of the Eastern Mediterranean. Wherever they had large scale commercial transactions we see them opening new commercial centers in order to facilitate import and export trade.

The Phoenicians
at Kition
Thus we see such a Phoenician trading center established at Kition. It's commercial value had been recognised for long, and it was here that an earlier Mycenaean city had flourished . It was possibly destroyed by an earthquake. The establishment of the Phoenician trading post here is dated to the early 9th century B.C. To start with it was a limited one but it expanded very fast and evolved into a Phoenician city where the Phoenicians brought their own gods - - Astarte, whose temple they built over the ruins of a Mycenaean temple, Melqart who was identified with Hercules, Reshef, who was identified with Apollo, and many others, worshipped in Syria, together with the mythology related to them. Thus Kition became a Phoenician religious, as well as cultural center which played a

very great influence on development of Cypriot religion, art, and culture from the 9th to the 7th centuries B.C. influencing other cities, and primarily Amathus.

Dominance of the sea by the Cypriots 742-709 B.C.
The activities of the Phoenicians spurred the interest of the Cypriots who had already established and strengthened their kingdoms. Now they turned their attention to commerce with the help of a strong fleet which gave them dominance over the sea for some 33 years, 742-709 B.C. Over the same period they renewed relations with the Hellenic world, and particulary with the islands and collaborated in establishing new colonies in Asia Minor and in Syria. Large quantities of Cycladic pottery of the 8th century B.C., discovered in Cypriot graves, testify to the tightening of relations.

Cyprus pays taxes and tribute to the Assyrians
The Assyrian king Sargon the Second put an and to the Cypriot domination of the sea when he conquered the island in 709 B.C. Records show us that seven, and later ten kings of Cyprus paid tribute and taxes to him in the form of gold, silver and timber. Such taxes continued to be paid upto the year 612 B.C., when the Assyrian empire collapsed when Nineveh fell to the Medes. This passage of the Assyrians through Cyprus left deep influences and traces upon Cypriot art and particularly on sculpture.

Relations with Athens - Solon in Cyprus
The period from 612 B.C., until the Egyptian incursions which started as piratical raids by Pharaoh Apries and ended in the island's conquest by his successor Pharaoh Amasis in 560 B.C., was a period of close relations with Athens. Since that time Athens has remained as a pole of attraction for the Cypriots. A visit to Cyprus by Lawgiver and sage Solon, indicates this turn towards Athens, as well as the increasing interest of Athens on Cyprus. Solon was the guest of king Philokypros who on Solon's advice moved his capital from Aipia to a newly founded city which he named Soli in honour of the Greek Statesman. It is during this period that Ionian sculpture so influences the sculpture of Cyprus.

Cypriot kings help Cyrus in his campaign against Babylon
The period during which Cypriot kings paid tribute to Egypt was comparatively short because over this very same period a new empire made its appearance in the East. This was the Persian empire which in 546 B.C. had already captured Sardis, thus adding the kingdom

The goblet and the askos, shaped like a bird are two examples of the development of Mycenaean art into the Cypro-geometric style. They were found together with a great number of others in graves of the final years of Late Bronze Age (11th century B.C.) at Alaas site near Gastria.

The Protogeometric era has provided us with a great abundance of ritual vessels (kernoi) like this one. It´s ring-like body has a bull and a goat's head connected to the body through a hole. It also has four miniature amphorae communicating with the interior. It was found at Rizokarpaso. 10th century B.C.

The "Hubbard" amphora is a representative example of pottery decoration at the end of the Geometric period. Human forms, animals, birds, and fish, all depicted in a free style are the main decorative motifs, which also continue into the Archaic era. 8th century B.C.

Amphora of the Cypro-Geometric III era from Chrysokhou. The pot´s neck is richly decorated in the free field style. Carts driven by cart drivers, galopping horses with riders, birds, a dog under the belly of a horse, all go to make up an artistic and harmonious whole.

of Croesos to his proffessions and eight years later, in 538 B.C. king Cyrus launched his great campaign against Babylon itself. Seeing this increasing power of the Persians, the kings of Cyprus correctly foresaw that the Persians would not overlook the island, which they had to control. In this way, they voluntarily chose to help Cyrus, hoping for a favourable treatment afterwards. Cyrus respected the authority of the kings of Cyprus who were allowed to pay tribute to the Great king, thus starting the Persian domination over the island.

Egyptian sculpture influnces Cypriot art   Alhtough short-lived, the passage of Egypt through Cyprus left strong traces on Cypriot art, and particularly on sculpture. This was the result of a custom of the Pharaoh Amasis, who sent Egyptian votive offerings to the temples of countries which he captured. It is certain that some of these votive offerings depicted the king himself. Some heads discovered, bear a clear Egyptian influence in technique. They could very well have been part of such votive offerings. It is also very likely that they were sculpted in Cyprus following the Egyptian influence upon Cypriot sculpture.

THE PERSIAN DOMINATION

Salamis pioneers - Evelthon   As mentioned, acceptance of Persian domination by the kings of Cyprus started in 538 B.C., when, voluntarily, they offered to help Cyrus the elder king of Persia, in his campaign against Babylon. The king of Salamis, Evelthon, pioneered in this and as a reward he was granted special influence and authority as testified by the silver coins which he was the first to mint bearing his name as the king of Cyprus, and not as the king of Salamis. In 530 B.C. he was visited by Queen Pheretime, mother of the exiled king of Cyrene, Askesilaos the third, who asked Evelthon to help reinstate her son. This is the second indication of Evelthon's power and influence over Cyprus. Salamis kept this power and influence throughout the Persian domination to such a degree that the history of Cyprus during this period is the history of the city of Salamis itself.

THE REVOLT OF ONESILOS

Ionian revolt
501-495 B.C.
The tyrant of Miletus, Aristagoras had fallen into the disfavour of King Darius who is seen as the organiser of the Persian Empire. In fear that he would be deprived of his authority . Aristagoras contacted the Hellenic cities of Asia Minor and incited a revolt against the Persians. He was very successful in this and the so-called Ionian revolt started in 501 B.C., and lasted six years.

Gorgos -
Onesilos
Gorgos, grandson of king Evelthon was on the throne of Salamis at that time, and he had every good reason to cultivate good relations with the Persians. His brother Onesilos, however, had visions of uniting Cyprus and liberating it from the Persians. He was, however, unable to convince Gorgos to join the Ionian revolt and was forced to dethrone him. Gorgos took refuge in the court of King Darius and convinced the Persian monarch to attack Onesilos, by revealing the plans for revolt.

Preparation for
revolt - Amathus
stance
Onesilos called upon the kings of Cyprus to act in unison and all agreed with the exception of the king of Amathus, and so Onesilos tried to capture the city in 498 B.C. He was unable to complete his plans, however, because he was forced to rush back to Salamis on information that the Persians had landed in the Karpas peninsula and were marching on the city under the command of Artyvios. Many believe that the refusal of Amathus to join Onesilos was due to the dominance of Phoenicians in the city, but there is no concrete evidence of this.

Cypriot defeat
betrayal by
Stasanor
The battle between the forces took place in the plain of Salamis. Onesilos personally fought Artyvios and slew him after his bodyguard lamed his horse. This feat, together with reports that the Ionian fleet had defeated and destroyed the Persian fleet off Salamis did strengthen the morale of the Cypriots. They would have won if the king of Kourion, Stasanor, who was followed by the Salaminian chariots did not desert to the camp of the Persians. Onesilos and his allies were thus defeated with Onesilos and the king of Soloi, Aristokypros both slain.

The importance of the revolt - the Onesilos legend   This end to the Onesilos revolt, which although it failled, underlined an important factor of the ensuing period. This is that Salamis became a center of attraction of Cyprus towards the Hellenic world with which, as was the case of the Ionian revolt, it fought many battles for liberty. This gave rise to the legend of Onesilos who was honoured as a hero by the oracle of Delphi. According to the legend, the Amathusians who fought with the Persians, wanting to revenge themselves on Onesilos, cut off his head and raised it on a pole in the city square. However, a swarm of bees occupied and made it into a bee hive. The Amathusians were afraid of this and asked the Oracle for advice. The oracle of Delphi advised that the head be buried with honours and that annual observances be held as fitting to a hero like Onesilos. Because it is known that all Cypriot inhabitants of pre-Hellenic descent concentrated in Amathus, and were known as the heteo-Cypriots, their acceptance of an oracle instructing a purely Hellenic hero-worship of Onesilos in a Hellenic liturgical form, gives the legend added significance and indicates the importance which Salamis gained as a Hellenic center. This city also had older relations with the oracle of Deplhi from the time when king Evelthon had donated a valuable incense burner to the oracle which was kept in the Corinthian Treasure House.

Consequences of the revolt   Very heavy consequences followed the failure of the revolt. Underlining the incorporation of the island within the Persian Empire, king Darius placed it, together with Phoenicia and Palestine within the Fifth Satrapy. After he restored Gorgos to the throne of Salamis, Darius saw to it that kings friendly to the Persian Empire were also installed in the other kingdoms. He even installed Phoenician kings in some of them, like in Idalion, and possibly in Lapithos and Marion, where the last king was also the king of Soloi. This is proved by numerous Marion coins found in the palace of Vouni near Soloi.

Conscription of Cypriots against the Ionians and Greece   One of the results of these arrangements was that Cypriots were conscripted into a Cypriot army, which was forced to fight against the Ionians, whose revolt was finally suppressed in 495 B.C. This conscription was repeated later, when Darius to start with, and then his successor Xerxes started their campaigns against Greece. In the Xerxes campaign the Cypriots were forced to provide 150 ships under the command of Gorgos of Salamis and his brother Philaon, who was captured by the Greeks in the naval battle near Artemi-

Herodotus informs us that war chariots were used in Cyprus until the 5th century B.C. It is for this reason that we often find images of war chariots in sanctuaries as votive gifts to the god of war. Here we have such an offering from Ovgoros. It has two warriors and a charioteer, from the sixth century B.C.

Here we have a painted idol of a horse with a rider 6th century B.C.

On either side of a huge bull we have two human figures whose head barely reaches the bull's back. In this way they stress their small size in face of the god of fertility and productivity. From an open-air sanctuary at Meniko. 6th century B.C.

By contrast to other depictions of centaurs, this multicoloured centaur has a quiver for arrows hanging from his shoulder. This underlines the character of the god worshipped in the sanctuary where it was found as a wargod 6th century B.C.

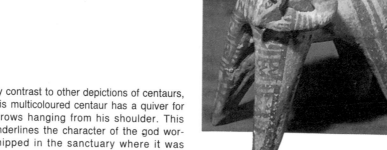

sion. Also in command were Timonactas, son of Timagoras and Penthilius of Paphos. However, in the naval battle of Salamis they were the first, together the Cilicians and the Egyptians, who turned tail, and became the primary reason for the defeat of the Persian fleet.

ATHENIAN OPERATIONS TO LIBERATE CYPRUS

First attemptunited Greeks to free Cyprus. Athens - Sparta dispute cause of failure

The destruction of the Persian fleet at Salamis in Greece, in 480 B.C., and the rout of the Persian army at Plataeai in 479 B.C., gave the initiative to the Greeks who then launched operations to free the islands and the Hellenic cities of Asia Minor. In the spring of 478 B.C. Pausanias, in command of a Hellenic fleet of 20 Peloponnesian and 30 Athenian triremes under Aristides and Kimon (Cimon) and assisted by additional triremes from the islands, set off for Cyprus. With the help of loyal inhabitants, he managed to free the cities. Their independence, however, was short lived. After the break-up of the Athens-Sparta alliance due to the treason of Pausanias, and his conviction to death, the Persians grasped the opportunity to recapture Cyprus and to reappoint kings who were faithfull to them in all the cities. The ambitions and the disputes among the Greeks led to the loss of a golden opportunity not only to liberate Cyprus, but also to destroy the Persian empire. This was attempted some 150 years later by Alexander the Great.

Kimon Asia Minor campaign

The treason of Pausanias undermined Greek confidence in Sparta and gave the Athenians the chance to become very powerful through their Athenian alliance. This alliance was formed to protect its member cities and the islands from Persian attacks, and to liberate Persian-held islands and the Hellenic cities of Asia Minor from the Persian yoke. The task was entrusted to Kimon. Commanding a fleet of 300 Athenian and allied triremes he launched an operation against the Asia Minor shores in 467 B.C. During this campaign, and in one single day Kimon managed to destroy a far superior Persian fleet, and on landing, to rout the Persian land forces near the mouth of the river Evrimedon. This double victory of Kimon was augmented with the destruction of a Phoenician fleet of 80 triremes off Cyprus, after it sailed to help the Persians. As a result, the Persians were forced to recognise the independence of some islands and cities, but these did not include Cyprus.

The Charitimides campaign   Eight years after the naval battle of Evrimedon, the Athenians and their allies launched a campaign for Cyprus under Charitimides in command of 200 triremes in 459 B.C. He did manage to liberate a number of cities in Cyprus but he broke off his campaign on orders from the Athenians to proceed to Egypt to support a revolt there against the Persians. The result was that with Charitimides departure, the Persians recaptured the lost cities with the help of the Phoenicians. An inscribed bronze tablet from Idalion refers to a murderous battle the target of which was the conquest of the city. This tablet was also the key to deciphering the Cypriot syllabic script. The tablet also states that honours were heaped upon doctor Onasilos, son of Onasikypros, because he treated all the wounded without charge.

Kimon in Cyprus   It is obvious that the recall of Charitimides was a very serious and unfortunate political error, and it was due to domestic squabbles between Athenian politicians. These squabbles led to the exile of Kimon in 461 B.C. and to adoption of the policy of his rival Pericles. Personal aspirations, once again, prevented the liberation of Cyprus. The Athenians did try to put things right in 450 B.C., when they recalled Kimon from exile and entrusted him with the liberation of Cyprus. They appointed general Anaxicrates as his assistant with 200 triremes. In face of Phoenician domination of the cities Kimon managed to destroy a combined Cilician and Phoenician fleet off Paphos. He captured Marion and liberated Soloi. He then turned to southern Cyprus intending to liberate Kition and then Salamis.

Kimon's death   During the siege of Kition and by a misfortune, Kimon fell ill and died before capturing the city in 449 B.C. In their effort to avoid confusion in the ranks of the army and navy, the generals concealed his death, and lifted the siege under the excuse of having to face a Phoenician fleet which moved against them. They did meet this fleet near Salamis and after defeating it they landed at Salamis and routed the Persian forces. The double victory was attributed to Kimon and thus created his posthumous motto: «though dead, he was victorious».

Athens - Persians peace. Cyprus abandoned   During the battle for Salamis the Athenians also lost the campaign's second in command, general Anaxicrates. Under these unfortunate conditions, they were forced to abandon the campaign and sign a peace with the Persians in 448 B.C. This not only left Cyprus to the Persians, but also abandoned it to its conquerors under much harsher conditions and treatment from the conquerors and their Phoenician allies.

National political
and cultural
significance of
operations

Although the efforts of the Athenians to free Cyprus were not successful, their significance is very great from various aspects, national , political and cultural. It has a national significance because of the common Greek and Cypriot blood shed in the battles for Cyprus. This was immortalised in the relief funerally stele found at Lysi and this common blood strengthened ties between Greece and Cyprus. Its political significance lies in the fact that Cyprus found itself in the Athenian alliance and the eclat of this fact reflected upon all aspects of life in Cyprus. It had it's cultural significance because it brought to Cyprus the influence and example of the magnificent civilization of the golden century of Pericles. The result was that a parallel civilization developed in Cyprus. Although the island had lost much of its personality in its lengthy past, under the light of this national unity, it was, once again, revitalised.

EVAGORAS THE FIRST

Salamis under
Phoenician
kings

Salamis was one of the cities that came under Phoenician kings after the failure of liberation attempts. Every possible effort was made to convert it to barbaric customs. The Phoenicians removed from the city everything that was Hellenic. By prohibiting the entry of Greeks into city they managed to put a stop to all the arts and commerce, and to stamp out cultural life. Misery and degradation reigned during this period. Even the pride and beliefs of the people were undermined. They resorted to the flattery of their oppressors in their effort to ease their own suffering. This gave rise to pro-Persian sentiments, which were further fanned with the advent of Avdimon to the throne in 415 B.C. According to Isocrates this Phoenician brought total barbarism to the city.

Evagoras takes
the throne

This was the state of affairs when, in 411 B.C., Evagoras appeared on stage. For unknown reasons he had not been banished from the city as were other members of the Teucrid royal family. He was twenty when Avdimon came to the throne. He immediately plotted to overthrow Avdimon. He travelled to Soloi of Cilicia where he formed a group of some 50 enthu-

The funerary stele of Aristila, mentioned in the text. Aristila is seated in an armchair. She wears a chiton and a pleated Himation. She is concentrating on a bird which she holds in her left hand. The manner in which she does this, automatically refers us to the stele of Hegiso which was lauded in a poem by Palamas. 5th century B.C.

Marion developed a tradition for a type of pots which bears plastically rendered decoration on the opposite side to the handle. Here we have a jug the spout of which is in the form of another jug held by a female figure. Both these elements are the pot's plastic decoration. 5th century B.C.

Another jug of the same type. Here the plastic decoration is made up of two female figures. In other examples of jugs of this type, the plastic decoration is a combination of Eros and Psyche. 4th century B.C.

siastic friends and followers, including some Athenians. When he considered the time right, he landed near Salamis, broke into the city walls at night, captured the palace and was then immediately recognised as king by the people.

First actions
by Evagoras
One of the first acts was to fortify the city thus creating confidence and security among the people.

His aim was to uproot the pro-Persian feelings and restore pro-Hellenic ones in their place by bolstering national pride. Towards this aim he opened the city's gates to the Athenians. Bearing in mind the support which Evagoras might give to them during the harsh days of the Peloponnesian war, the Athenians responded and cultivated free contact and communication between the cities of Athens and Salamis. It is during this period that orator Andocides and sophist Polycrates, among numerous others, chose to settle in Salamis. Encouraging Evagoras' initiatives, the Athenians proclaimed him a citizen of Athens only a year after he took over the throne. Thus very soon Salamis regained its old glory and rhythm, and became the center of the arts and of learning, and spread its beneficial influence over the other cities of the island.

Evagoras and
Konon
The close ties of Evagoras with Athens, were further cemented by the arrival at Salamis of general Konon. After the calamity of the Aigos Potamoi naval battle, the general, together with eight ships took refuge at Salamis and became the guest of Evagoras. The great friendship which developed between the two men had a great benefit on both sides. Under the encouragement of Konon, Evagoras developed friendly relations with Artaxerxes, who recognised Evagoras as the king of Salamis. Artaxerxes provided Evagoras and Konon with the sum of 500 talents for construction of a fleet of 100 triremes which were armed and manned by Athenians. In command of this fleet in 394 B.C. Konon defeated Sparta at Knidos and put an end to Spartan command of the seas.

Athenian honours
for Evagoras
The victory at Knidos was widely attributed to Evagoras. Honours were heaped upon him by the Athenians. They raised a statue in his honour. Together with a statue of Konon, they were placed side by side in the «Stoa (Portico) Vasilios» in Athens. He was also honoured with a wreath of olive branches in a proclamation read during the Dionysian games. He and his discendents were given a seat of honour at these Dionysian games.

Cyprus under Evagoras' autority   Evagoras aspired to unite all the kingdoms of Cyprus under his own scepter so that together, and united, they might campaign against the Persians in order to liberate the whole island. Over a period of twenty years, and thanks to his wise policies, he was recognised by all the kings of the island voluntarily except for those of Kition, Amathus and Soloi, which he tried to subdue. He asked for help from the Athenians who sent him 10 triremes and 800 light troops under the command of Chavrias. They landed on the island in 387 B.C., and the united forces of Evagoras and the Athenians captured Kition, then Amathus and Soloi, and in less than one year the whole island was under Evagoras in 387 B.C.

Peace of Antalcidas - 386 B.C.   Things changed, however, one year later, when the Athenians recalled Chavrias, leaving Evagoras to his own resources, and relying on his own strength. The Spartans, fearing the ever increasing might of Athens, which dominated the sea after its naval victory at Knidos, signed a treaty with Artaxerxes, known as the Antalcidas peace. Under this treaty Sparta recognised Persian sovereignty over the islands and cities that Persia held. Under the conditions of the treaty, anyone who violated it would be considered an enemy of the Great King, as well as an enemy of Sparta. The Athenians were thus forced to follow the terms of the treaty. The Athens - Sparta conflict, once again became the obstacle to a re-unification of the Hellenes in a struggle against the Persian empire.

Evagoras preparations   Against all difficulties, Evagoras did not give up his efforts to liberate the island. After getting substantial help from the Egyptian king Akoris, who had also rebelled against the Persians and won substantial victories, Evagoras built a fleet of 90 ships, armed an army of six thousand men, and with the help of other participating cities and mercenaries he attacked the Phoenicians and captured Tyre. At the same time, he managed to incite Cilicia to revolt. It was at this juncture that Artaxerxes decided to move against Evagoras. He appointed Orontes and Tyrivazos as commanders of his campaign.

First operations   In 385 B.C. Orontes landed near Kition and a part of his army marched on the city. Evagoras reacted with speed. After defeating the Persians on land, he managed to surprise the patrolling Persian fleet and destroyed a number of ships. When the Persians recovered from their surprise, they re-deployed their forces and forced the fleet of Evagoras to flee. They also forced Evagoras himself to seek refuge within the city walls of Salamis. The Persians then started a siege of the city from land as well as from the sea.

War's end   The siege of Salamis, and the war, went on for years. The entire military adventure, however, ended with an honourable peace signed in 379 B.C. which was reached through protracted negotiations between Evagoras and Tirivazos, to begin with, and then between Evagoras and Orontes according to the conditions of which, Evagoras was forced to free all the kingdoms of Cyprus, confine himself to being the king of Salamis alone, and to pay an annual tribute to the Great King, as a king to a king.

The significance of the wars of Evagoras   At first glance, it appears that the wars of Evagoras, which went on for years, failed to achieve the goal of this great visionary, that is to unite the island under him, and thus under this unification, to force the Persians to give up their sovereignty. However, although Evagoras failed to gain his main goal, his wars brought other benefits. Artaxerxes was humiliated. Before Evagoras, no Persian king had ever signed a treaty with any subject in revolt before this subject had capitulated and was punished. In the case of Evagoras, not only was there a signed treaty, but the rebel king was also recognised as an equal of his soverign. This very recognition was the first political defeat of the Persians and a very important political victory for Evagoras. Another very great and important achievement was that the wars of Evagoras put a final end to any attempt by the Persians and their Phoenician allies to barbarise Cyprus. From now on the Persians remained satisfied with collecting their taxes, without any interference in the administration of the local kings.

Foundations of national spirit   The third, and perhaps the most important achievement, was that the wars of Evagoras created a national spirit and brought Cypriot Hellenism much closer to the Hellenic center. In this way the Hellenic civilization was rekindled and was brought from Athens to the most important Hellenic center in Cyprus, to Salamis. The works of art from this period, discovered in Salamis and other cities, are inestimable treasures reflecting Hellenic art in the most classical forms. It became clear that after Evagoras, no power on earth could deflect the orientation of Cyprus towards the rest of the Hellenic world.

If this marble head of Aphrodite had been found in Athens, nobody would have had any hesitation in attributing it to Praxiteles or to Skopas. It is, however, the work of an artist from Salamis which demonstrates a very strong Hellenic influence. It is from the 4th century B.C., and illustrates the beneficial influence upon art as it was made possible by the opening offered by Evagoras the First, towards Athens.

A silver stater of Evagoras the First, who was the first to use Greek characters on a coin. On one side, on the left, a head of Hercules, and on the other, on the right, a deer.

One side of a silver stater of the 5th century B.C., with the head of a Gorgon from Soloi. On the other side it had an angry lion.

Evagoras coins. Use of the Greek alphabet   The Hellenic policy of Evagoras achieved all this, but it also influenced writing itself. Before him, all inscriptions on Cypriot coins were in the Cypriot syllabic script. This illustrated the very conservative character of the Cypriot kings. Evagoras was the first to use characters from the Greek alphabet which started to replace the Cypriot syllabic script from his time. Although a subject king to the Great Persian king, Evagoras was also the first Cypriot king to mint his own gold coins. Only the Great King of Persia had such a privilege. Generally, the coins minted by Evagoras were modelled on Greek patterns with the images of gods and heroes inscribed on their surfaces.

Murder of Evagoras   Evagoras dedicated the rest of his life to peace, without wars, and to peaceful projects. His efforts towards cultural development did continue with the same zeal with the same results. He lived for six more years after the end of his wars, only to meet a truly miserable end. Both he, and his first born son, Pnytagoras, were assassinated and the throne passed to his second son, Nicocles. There is no question that his death left a vacuum. Unquestionably, Evagoras was the strongest personality in Cypriot history. His wisdom, combined to his bravery, patriotism and steel-like will brought reform to Salamis and with it, it brought reform to Cypriot Hellenism. Recognising these qualities of Evagorism, Isocrates elevated him to the ranks of the heroes and semigods and considered him able to govern not only over Cyprus, but also over the whole of Asia.

THE SUCCESSORS OF EVAGORAS

Nicocles 374-361 B.C.   Nicocles, Evagoras' second son, was described by Isocrates, who was his teacher, in two speeches, which advised the young man to follow in this father's footsteps so that he may become a worthy successor to Evagoras. Nicocles, however, proved his Athenian orator-tutor wrong. Having a bent for wealthy good living, he fell into bad company and was led astray by king Straton of Sidon. They had become good friends and started a life of debauchery, disgusting the people, who, in the end dethroned him and cast him into prison, where he died.

Evagoras the second 361-331 B.C.   Nicocles was succeeded by Evagoras the second who was strongly pro-Persian at a time when even the Phoenicians themselves revolted against

Persia. At this very same period, the other kings decided to act in unison against the Persians, but Evagoras the second refused. The people deposed him and put Pnytagoras on the throne in his place. He was a grandson of Evagoras the first and the peoples' mandate to him was that he should join the other kings against the Persians.

Pnytagoras - third revolt against Persia

Responding to the peoples' mandate Pnytagoras did join the other kings, who accepted him as the leader of the revolt. The Persian king Artaxerxes the third, the Ochus, egged on by the deposed Evagoras the second, who had taken refuge in his court, ordered the Satrap of Caria to raise an army and a fleet in order to campaign against the revolutionaries. A force of eight thousand men and forty ships under Evagoras the second and an Athenian general, Fokion, did land on the North shores of Cyprus and marched against Salamis which they besieged, after pillaging the surrounding countryside without meeting any resistance. The other kings of the island did not resist, even though they could have crushed such a small force with their combined might. The siege of Salamis dragged on and Artaxerxes, who was faced with more serious dangers from other quarters, was forced to sign a treaty with Pnytagoras as king of Salamis. He was satisfied with the payment of taxes in the very same way Evagoras the first had done. Evagoras the second was appointed satrap of Phoenicia but he behaved so badly that the Phoenicians chased him out. He sought refuge in Salamis, where he was arrested and executed.

Alexander the Great - Cyprus fleet at the siege of Tyre

The reign of Pnytagoras coincided with the campaign of Alexander the Great against the Persian empire. Possessing the attributes of his grandfather, Evagoras the first, Pnytagoras convinced the other kings to support Alexander and help him with their combined fleets which were a considerable force. This was done after the great victory of the Macedonians at Issus in 333 B.C. Pnytagoras himself with Androcles of Paphos, Pasicrates of Soloi and other kings, not mentioned by name, placed 120 ships at the Macedonian's disposal. This fleet under admiral Andromachus besieged Tyre and in the end vanquished it in 332 B.C. At the same time many Cypriots joined the army of Alexander the Great and it is established that in the campaign in India, his general Nearchus, used Cypriots Phoenicians and Egyptians as rowers in crossing the river Indus.

Alexander honours Cyprus   The conduct of the Cypriots led Alexander the Great to honour and grant intependence to the kings of Cyprus, and to reward them. To king Pnytagoras, specifically, he granted the mines of Tamassos which had been owned by the Phoenicians. Other Cypriots were appointed to important posts by Alexander. Among them are mentioned Nicocles, son of the king of Soloi who was named chief of the triremes; Stasanor who was appointed governor of the provinces Aria and Drangiani. Another distinction was that Alexander entrusted Cypriot king Nicocreon, who succeded Pnytagoras, to be king of Salamis, and king Pasicrates of Soloi to be choregoi in a dramatic contest which was part of Alexander's celebrations for his victories over the Persians.

Conclusions on Persian domination of Cyprus   The Persian sovereignty over Cyprus was finally put to an end when the Cypriots joined forces with Alexander the Great and when they were given their own autonomy by the Macedonian leader. This Persian domination had continued for two entire centuries described as the period with the strongest political upheavals which in turn gave rise to, and created, the Hellenic conscience of the Cypriots as a result of joint struggles for independence. The failure of the Persians to strengthen their dominance is specifically due to the increase of national feeling of the people who dethroned kings in order to strengthen and support ties forged in common and joint struggles and sacrifices. The flowering of the arts and learning within purely Hellenic boundaries was the strongest resistance to the barbarization of the island. In this way, it can be said that the Persians did contribute spiritually and culturally to the unification of the island to the rest of the Hellenic world, and particularly with Athens.

Hellenic and Eastern influences are combined on this beautiful amphora. Under the neck the Sphinxes are of an Eastern technique. Each one faces the other with the sacred tree between them. The meander hooks below show an Hellenic influence. 7th century B.C.

The handles on this footed crater depict the heads of bulls. The lotus flowers on the leck, also demonstrate an Eastern influence while the rest of the decoration is purely of a Hellenic island influence.

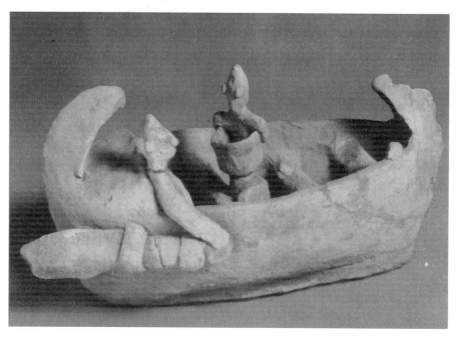

There is great variety of the subject matter which the Cypriot artist copied in clay, making votive and sacred offerings to sanctuaries. Here we have a model of a ship with its crew. It was found at Klirou. 7th to the 6th centuries B.C.

CYPRUS AND THE PTOLEMIES

Strategic importance of Cyprus   The untimely death of Alexander the Great created very many problems among the generals who succeeded him. Each one of them started seeking allies in order to strengthen their personal authority over specific countries and regions. From this point of view Cyprus could be a very strong ally, not only because of its strategic position, but also due to its still extensive and lush forests which were able to offer ample timber for shipbuilding. It is for this very reason that Alexander's successors vied with each other in their efforts to keep the island for themselves.

Ptolemy Lagos   The first who tried to occupy and hold the island, was the satrap of Egypt, Ptolemy Lagos. His sovereignty was voluntarily accepted by four of the kings of Cyprus - Nicocreon of Salamis, Androcles of Amathus, Nicocles of Paphos, and Pasicrates of Soloi. With the help of these four, he managed to convince the other kings to recognise him and accept his sovereignty over them.

Antigonus   Ptolemy's efforts were not very successful because four of the other kings, Pygmalion of Kition, Praxippos of Lapithos, Stasioikos of Marion, and Themison of Kerynia, sided with Antigonus who was the satrap of Greater Phrygia. After protracted efforts he managed to overthrow all the other satraps of Asia Minor, as well as the all-powerful satrap Evmenios, and thus proclaimed himself the Satrap of the whole of Asia Minor.

Ptolemy master of Cyprus   The news of the alliance between the four and Antigonous angered Prolemy who mastered a force of 13 thousand men and 100 ships, also supported by Selefkos, and under the command of Ptolemy's brother Menelaus, he soon managed to capture Lapithos as well as Kerynia, occupy Marion, and force Kition to come to terms. The two-year operation, 316-315 B.C. thus placed the entire island under the sovereignty of Ptolemy.

Nicocreon and Axiothea - the end of the Teucrid dynasty. Abolition of royalty

New irregularities emerged, forcing Ptolemy to take harsh measures, first against Pygmalion, the last king of Kition, whom he executed. He then sacked the city and razed its temples because it was considered a center of Phoenician religious worship. He then acted against Nicocreon of Salamis, whose tragic end was described by Diodorus the Sicilian. According to this narrative, Ptolemy first sent an army against Nicocreon whom he accused of plotting against him. Not wanting to surrender to Ptolemy, Nicocreon preferred to commit suicide and his example was followed by his wife Axiothea and other members of his family. This put an end to the Teucrid dynasty in 311 B.C., and with the end of the dynasty all the other kingdoms were abolished in 310 B.C. Cyprus this came under the absolute administration of the Ptolemies, with Menelaus, Ptolemy's brother, as the first ruler. The tomb of Nicocreon, with his tragic terracotta image, was discovered not long ago. There is one version, according to which this tragic story does not refer to Nicocreon, but to Nicocles of Paphos. However, the first version is accepted as the most certain.

Demetrius the besieger in Cyprus

The final clash, which brought Cyprus under total occupation by Ptolemy, occurred four years later in 306 B.C. Antigonus sent his son, Demetrius, with a force of 15 thousand infantry, 400 cavalry, 100 triremes and 54 other ships to capture the island. The force landed at Urania, in the Karpass peninsula and marched on Salamis. The city was besieged after the army of Menelaus, which waited outside the walls, was vanquished. During this siege, Demetrius had used siege machinery of his own invention, and for this he became known as the besieger. One of these machines, known as Elepolis, was 45 cubits wide and 90 cubits high, and had nine platforms, each one of which was equipped with its own siege apparatus and catapults, and was manned by 200 men. With the help of these machines he managed to destroy a great part of the city walls, but he failed to capture the city itself.

Defeat of Ptolemy Occupation of Cyprus by Demetrius

In his effort to help Menelaus, Ptolemy rushed with 140 triremes, 200 cargo ships and ten thousand men. In a decisive naval battle which took place between Salamis and Kition, Ptolemy's force was routed. Of his fleet, 80 triremes were destroyed and another 40 with 100 cargo ships and eight thousand men surrendered to Demetrius. The siege of Salamis was tightened after this naval engagement. With Demetrius' victory, Menelaus had no other choice. He surrendered and handed over the city. Other cities then followed the example of Salamis and all of Cyprus came under the sovereignty of Antigonus who crowned himself king of Cyprus and ruled until 301 B.C. when he was killed in the battle of the successors at Ipsos.

Final victory of the Ptolemies
After the death of Antigonus Cyprus remained under the sovereignty of his son, Demetrius who held onto the island because he needed its fleet so that he could carry out his own aspirations, He used the fleet in his campaign against the Peloponnese in 295 B.C., when he tried to capture it. His absence from the island, however, gave the opportunity to Ptolemy Soter the First, to recapture Cyprus the very next year without any difficulty. This started the reign of the Ptolemies in 294 B.C., and it continued until 58 B.C.

THE REIGN OF THE PTOLEMIES (294-58 B.C.)

Ptolemy Philadelphus - Arsinoe
During the reign of the Ptolemies, Cyprus took part in all the adventures of the kings of Egypt. Ptolemy Soter the first was succeded by Ptolemy Philadelphus whose name is connected to the establishment of new cities, which he named after his wife Arsinoe. He rebuilt Marion which had been destroyed by Ptolemy the First. He renamed it Arsinoe. He then built another city near Salamis and gave it the same name. It has survived as today's Famagusta.

Ptolemy Philometor and Antiochus the 4th, the Prominent
Under Ptolemy Philometor, Cyprus got embroiled in many adventures because of the conflict between him and his brother Ptolemy the Benefactor the 2nd who is better known under the name of Fyskon. The result of one of these adventures was the capture of the island by Antiochus the 4th, known as the Prominent, who was the king of Syria, in 168 B.C. However, he was forced to give it up very soon thanks to the intervention of the Romans.

Ptolemy Fyskon, Aristarchos Samothrax
Ptolemy Fyskon ascended the throne of Egypt by marrying Cleopatra the Second, widow of Ptolemy Philometor. An evil man by nature, he persecut-

This head of a statue is not made of marble which would have justified its fineness. It is made of limestone on which it is difficult for the artist to depict detail and illustrate his inner sentiments. And yet this piece of art work is one of the finest and most beautiful examples of Cypriot art, in which the artist has managed to give the Hellenic character and to create a masterpiece, using a baser form of material. It was found at Arsos. 3rd century B.C.

An excellent head of a kore, made of limestone. The light smile demonstrates the Ionic influence while the rich and plaited hairdo strongly illustrates the local colour. Found at Dali, 5th century B.C.

ed the men of letters, many of whom were forced to leave Egypt. One of them was the renowned Aristarchos Samothrax, scholiast of Homer and director of the famous library of Alexandria. He came over to Cyprus where he died.

Ptolemy Lathyros   Cyprus was involved in yet more such adventures under Ptolemy Lathyrus. After a series of under-handed plots in which Cleopatra was involved, Lathyrus was forced to leave Egypt, passing on the throne to his younger brother Alexander. He came to Cyprus and was proclaimed king in 106 B.C. Later on (88 B.C.) Alexander was chased out of Alexandria, came to Cyprus, and was slain in a battle. In this way the throne of Egypt reverted to Lathyrus and Cyprus was once more united with Egypt under one throne.

Ptolemy Auletes   On the death of Lathyrus in 80 B.C. the conflict over succession increased and the king of Cyprus, Ptolemy Auletes was in the end proclaimed king of Egypt and ruled until 58 B.C., when the island was captured by the Romans.

Organization of the state   As mentioned earlier, Ptolemy the 1st abolished the kingdoms of Cyprus in 310 B.C., and he had appointed a supreme governor with administrative and military command over the island. Because of the island's great and important strategic value, and because it supplied timber and all other means for construction of fleets, the Ptolemies saw to it that the organization of the state was on a purely military basis.

Transfer of the capital - Paphos   On abolishing the kingdoms, Ptolemy the 1st transferred the island's capital to Paphos. Paphos was closer and more accessible to Egypt, and the Paphos area boasted of much richer timber - yielding resources from its thick forests. At the same time, the rulers were extremely fond of hunting, and the Paphos forests were also rich in game. This transfer gave Paphos a special eclat and scintillation, because of the wealth it amassed. This is clearly proved by recent archeological excavations.

General, General-emperor Lieutenant General   A General was the island's supreme ruler and he was directly responsible to the king of Egypt, whose authority he exercised in a very totalitarian manner. He was exclusively responsible for, and had the authority, to mint coins and was in charge of the mint. In case of dangers from the outside his authority was absolute and unlimited. In such instances he took on the title of General-Emperor and there are records indicating he could appoint lieutenant Generals in-chief as his assistants.

High Priest -
Admiral
When Ptolemy the Prominent was the king of Egypt, he added to the authorities of the General, the duties of High Priest in 203 B.C. He did this in his effort to increase royal revenues since the wealth of the temples and particularly that of the Temple of Aphrodite, became vast. A short time later, Ptolemy Fyskon added the duties of Admiral to those of the General. This became necessary because Cyprus had acquired a special naval importance after the defeat of Greece by the Romans in 146 B.C., and secondly pirates attacking from Asia Minor and the islands, were ravaging the Mediterranean. Thus it became essential to strengthen the authority of the General enabling him to deal with the situation much more effectively.

Other authorities
The second highest post was held by the «secretary» who served under the direct orders of the General. Then there were the «Hegemones» or Commanders-in-chief and the «Ipparchoi» in command of army units. City administrators were called «overseers» and they held both administrative as well as military positions. The chief builder or «architect» was responsible for the construction as well as the maintenance of the fleet, and this was also a military position. There were also a number of other positions such as that of the chief of metals, the chief of hunters and a number of others usually entrusted to men under the favour of the Ptolemies.

Koinon Kyprion
On many plinths (=bases) for statues there are dedicatory inscriptions not from a single person but from «The Koinon Kyprion» (The Confederacy of Cypriots). Since these dedications were usually to Generals or other military officers, it is believed that «TheKoinon Kyprion» comprises the whole of the Cypriot army which with other military units of mercenaries made up the army of the General of the island or the king. In other inscriptions there are references of «Koinon Achaion», «Koinon Thrakon» etc. who certainly were mercenaries.

Demos, Vouli,
Gerousia
One could expect that the Ptolemies, with their military organization and structure of administration, would have suppressed every freedom of the local populace, ruling them in a totalitarian manner. Things, however, were

Left: A limestone statue of exceptional importance, because of the relief depictions of the symbols of Egyptian worship seen on the dress. It was found in the sanctuary of Serapis at Soloi. 4th century A.D.

Right: A huge and headless marble statue of Asklepios, which, together with a great number of others, they decorated the stoas of the Salamis gymnasium. It belongs to the Hellenistic times. 4th to the 3rd century B.C.

very different in fact. Inscriptions inform us that some form of independence was maintained in domestic administration. The cities possessed the «demos» (popular assembly), the «vouli» (council) and the «Gerousia» (senate) institutions unknown and new in Cyprus, but as institutions they had been established and functioned in the Hellenic world much earlier.

Gymnasia
Gymnasiarchs

Apart from these three city institutions, a fourth one was introduced to Cyprus. This was the institution of the Gymnasium and the Gymnasiarchos. The latter was responsible for the athletic as well as the spiritual training and preparation of the youth. Gymnasia excavated at Salamis and Kition, but particularly the one at Salamis, with the wealth of artifacts discovered, testify to the great importance attributed to these institutions. Such gymnasia existed in all the cities, Paphos, Arsinoe, Kurion, Lapithos, Chytri, and elsewhere as proved by inscriptions found.

Religious
influences

The worship of Egyptian deities, is, very naturally, related to the capture and the administration of Cyprus by the Ptolemies. In a number of cities, excavations have revealed temples dedicated to the gods of Egypt, such as Isis, Osiris, and Serapis. It is also known that the Ptolemies, like all Egyptian pharaohs, were proclaimed gods upon their death and their statues were also placed in the temples. It was very natural that this religious practice was also brought to Cyprus where we often find statues, or plinths (basis for a statue), with Ptolemaic inscriptions. We also find areas devoted to their worship. The worship of Arsinoe was well known. She was identified to Aphrodite and places of worship for Arsinoe were found both in Paphos as well as in Arsinoe near Salamis, and Idalion. Generally the religion of Egypt left very deep marks in Cyprus, particularly during the Ptolemaic era.

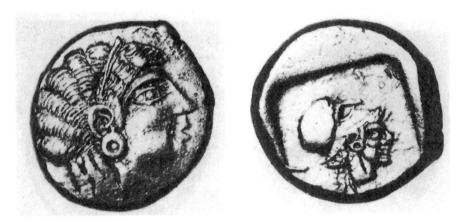

A silver stater of 480 B.C., from Lapithos. On the left we have Aphrodite with wavy hair. On the right we have Athena with a helmet in the Corinthian style.

A silver stater of the 5th century B.C., of King Stasioikos of Marion. On one side we have Apollo crowned with laurel. On the right we have Aphrodite on the back of a galopping bull.

Silver stater from 460 B.C. of Idalion. On one side it has a Sphinx with a curved wing, and on the other side a lotus flower.

One side of a silver stater from Amathus (375 B.C.).
On both sides it has a lion with open jaws.

Two sides of a silver stater of the 4th century B.C. from Kition. On the left we have Hercules wearing the lion´s skin on his head and shoulders and on the right a lion on top of a deer ready to tear it apart.

One side of a silver stater of the 4th century B.C. from Paphos.
It has an eagle´s head on the other side.

General view of the Gymnasium at Salamis. The Corinthian style capitals of the columns are very clearly visible.

ROMAN ERA

**Conquest
by Cato**
After the destruction of Carthage, and the conquest of Greece, the Romans turned their attention to Egypt and Cyprus. They had very often interfered in the domestic affairs of both these countries and what they needed was simply an excuse to set their plans into motion. In the case of Cyprus the truly unimportant excuse was provided by Puplius Claudius the Beautiful, a political friend of Julius Caesar. He was captured by pirates who asked for 50 talents in order to release him. The king of Cyprus, Ptolemy Auletes, refused to lend Claudius the money when requested by him to do so. After his eventual liberation, Claudius became the Tribune of Rome and managed to extract a vote from the Senate, declaring Cyprus a Roman district. Enforcement of the decision was entrusted to Marcus Porcius Cato, who captured the island without meeting any serious resistance in 58 B.C.

**Ptolemies' wealth
goes to Rome**
Acting on a second Senate decision after the conquest of the island, Cato confiscated the entire property of Ptolemy, who had in the meantime committed suicide. This huge property included items of immense value such as precious stones, royal goblets, purple clothes and much else. All of it was taken to Rome, where it was put up for sale by auction. It brought a total of seven thousand talents, and this sum went into the state coffers of Rome. Apart from this wealth, Cato also took with him to Rome a large number of slaves, as well as a statue of Zeno of Kition which he kept for himself, being a follower of this philosopher's teaching.

**The first
governors**
As a province, Cyprus was joined to Cilicia which was captured by Rome in 103 B.C., and the island was administered by local governors appointed by the proconsuls. The first such governors were only interested in making more money. There is reference to Salamis, which was granted a loan with an interest of 48 percent, instead of the legal 12 percent and it became necessary for Cicero, who was appointed proconsul in 51 B.C., to

intervene and stave off a calamity facing the senators who had signed for the loan. Cicero was the first such proconsul to show a protective interest for the Cypriots.

Octavian Augustus and the rise of Paphos   When Octavian Augustus became Emperor of Rome, Cyprus was subdivided into four districts- Salamis, Paphos, Amathus and Lapithos. This division remained in force into the times of Byzantium. Under Augustus, Paphos, which had been maintained as the capital, gained much prominence, fame, as well as wealth. When the city was destroyed by earthquake in 17 or 15 B.C., Augustus showed a great interest in it and even provided monetary aid for the citizens and gave the city the name of "Sevasti" or the revered one. On an inscription we can read the name "Sebasti, Claudia, Flavia Paphos, sacred metropolis of the cities of Cyprus."

The Jewish rebellion   Under the Roman rule Cyprus did not show any historic development of its own, because it was so closely attached to Roman history. For this reason there will be mention only of those events which had a specific significance to the island and which, for this reason, are very limited. The first such event was the Jewish rebellion in 116 A.D., when Trajan was emperor of Rome. There was a great number of Jews on the island, and the Romans entrusted them with the operation of the mines. It is recorded that in 12 B.C., Augustus, had granted King Herod the privilage of exporting half the production from Soloi mines for a price of 300 talents. The Jewish revolution was directed by Artemion and it is said that some 240 thousand Jews and Cypriots died in it. Even though the number can be an exaggeration, it shows that the population of Cyprus was, perhaps greater than today.

Attack by the Goths   The raids by Goths against Roman provinces, including Cyprus, around 269 A.D., must be considered of special significance. It is on record that the Goths in Cyprus fell victims to various diseases, and they were forced to abandon the island before causing any serious damage.

The Kalokairos revolution   When Contantine the Great remained the sole Emperor of Byzantium, after his great victory over Licinius, the second Emperor, and Masxentius outside Rome, he sent Kalokairos to Cyprus as Governor. He helped the is-

Clay portraits of four men and one woman were found in the debris and ashes of a great fire above a royal cenotaph at Salamis. They are identified as portraits of King Nikokreon and Axiothea and their family, who committed suicide in 311 B.C. Perhaps here we have the portrait of the last of the line of the Teucridae which resembles the style of Lysippos.

From very early times the fame of the temple of Aphrodite at Paphos had spread far beyond Cyprus and spread to the surrounding area. The Ptolemies as well as the Romans helped spread this fame which was very profitable . The Romans used the temple as a dominant feature on coins, as we see it on this coin of Vespasian. The representation of the temple with its cone, the symbol of her worship, must be true representation of its architecture.

A copper miniature of Zeus Amon of the 3rd century B.C., from Soloi. The eyes are inset with silver. The beard is curly and the hair forms two horns. These two features testify to the identity of the god, whose worship was introduced by the Ptolemies.

A limestone head in natural size so finely produced that it could be a portrait. It is believed to be the head of Caligula (37-41 A.D.)

land overcome the privations and misery caused by earthquakes and long droughts. There is also a legend that he imported to Cyprus large numbers of cats of a special breed to combat the vipers which had greatly multiplied because of the long droughts. It is said that Cavo Gata, the cape of cats, got it´s name from that time, because the cats were released on that cape. He is also credited with the construction of the Monastery of Saint Nicholas of the Cats on the said cape. Kalokairos, however, wanted to take Cyprus out of the Roman empire for his own interests, and this forced Constantine to send his nephew Dalmatius, who suppressed the revolution in 333 A.D.

City destruction by earthquakes The earthquakes and the long drought, which brought privation to the island have already been mentioned. It is a recorded fact that a great number of such earthquakes did strike the island causing havoc and great damage . It is considered certain that Engomi and Kition were abandoned after being completely destroyed by earthquake. Another such earthquake destroyed Paphos in 17 B.C. The city had been rebuilt by Augustus. Paphos was again destroyed, together with two others, Salamis and Kition, by another earthquake in 78 A.D. during the reign of Emperor Vespasian. Another strong earthquake hit Salamis in 332 A.D. The city was, once again, destroyed by an even stronger earthquake ten years later, and it was rebuilt by the son of Constantine, Flavius Constanine. The city was renamed Constantia in his honour and once again became the capital of Cyprus after Paphos was once again destroyed by an earthquake at about the same time. From that time on Paphos went into a deep decline.

The great drought and Sainte Helene A very long drought preceded these earthquakes and some historians say it lasted for 17, and others, 36 years. Famine decimated the people, many of whom were forced to leave the island. Legend connects the end of the drought with the arrival on the island of Sainte Helene in 327 A.D., on her return from the Holy Land, where she had discovered the Holy Cross. Sainte Helene showed a great interest and compassion in the island and in her desire to help the people, she built the Monastery of Stavrovouni to which she donated a piece of the Holy Cross. According to the legend and because of this act, the heavens did open up with torrential rains. This caused the rivers to flow, once again, including the river near the mouth of which Sainte Helene had landed. Since that time it is called the Vasilikos Potamos (Royal River), and the place is known as Vasiliko to this day. Sainte Helene donated pieces of the Holy Cross to two more Monasteries, at Tochni and Omodos, which treasure this legacy to the present day.

Koinon Kyprion　　　According to numerous inscriptions, the Romans did not abolish all administrative freedom. In many cities they maintained the Vouli and the demos- the council and the popular assembly, which were first established under the Ptolemies. In Salamis we also have mention of a senate. The "Koinon Kyprion" (Confederacy of Cypriots) was also maintained but now it did not represent a military unit as under the Ptolemies. It now represented all Cypriots, as a political and religious entity which, since the reign of Emperor Claudius in 44 A.D., was given the right to mint its own coins in copper with the inscription "Koinon Kyprion." A large number of such coins are still in existence.

CHRISTIANITY ON CYPRUS

Apostles Paul and　　　In the fourth year of the reign of Emperor Claudi-
Barnabas　　　us, in 45 A.D., the apostles Paul and Barnabas arrived on the island, and they were accompanied by Mark the Evangelist. After preaching the Lord's Word in Salamis, as well as in other cities, which then had a Hebrew population, they arrived in Paphos, which at that time was the seat of the Roman Proconsul Sergius Paulus who was the first to be converted by Apostle Paul. The conversion followed a great miracle performed on the magician Elima, who was first blinded and then cured. This miracle and the fact that the proconsul was the first to be baptized into Christianity, encouraged many Cypriots to convert and become Christians.

Martyrdom by　　　The two apostles left the island after first organis-
Apostle Barnabas　　ing the church and appointing bishops. Apostle Barnabas returned later and became the Bishop of Salamis. During the persecution of the Christians by Emperor Nero, Barnabas was captured by the Jews of the city and was then subjected to martyrdom. According to the «Acts of the Apostles» he was then buried by his nephew Mark the Evangelist, who also placed on the chest of Barnabas a hand written manuscript of the Gospel by Mathew. The remains of Apostle Barnabas, together with the Gospel were discovered by Anthemios, Bishop of Constantia in 485 A.D.

The first bishops　　　The first bishop to be ordained by Apostles Paul and Barnabas, was Heraklidios, Bishop of Tamassos, where his monastery still stands today. Bishop Heraklidios, acting on orders from Apostle Paul, ordained Epaphras as Bishop of Paphos. Under Paul's instructions. Tychikos was ordained Bishop of Neapolis, today's Limassol, and Auxibius was ordained Bishop of Soloi by St. Mark the Evangelist. Saint Lazarus must be mentioned here. After his resurrection, he came to Cyprus and was ordained Bishop of Kition, a see which he served for thirty years.

The First
Oecumenical
Synod -
St. Spyridon

Despite the heavy persecution to which it was subjected, the Church of Cyprus produced a number of saints and many prominent bishops. At the first Ecumenical Synod at Nicaea in 325 A.D., Cyprus was respresented by three bishops, Cyril of Paphos, Gelasius of Salamis, and Spyridon of Tremithus. Spyridon was to become the famous saint who was martyred, and eventually buried in his see. In 688 A.D. the remains of Saint Spyridon were taken to Constantinople, in no way affected by time, and in 1453 the same remains were taken to the island of Corfu (Kerkyra) where they remain to this day. From that time Spyridon became the protector saint of Corfu, and one of the greatest Cypriot saints.

Monastic life
Saint Hilarion

Monastic life flourished in Cyprus since the fourth century after Christ. Monasteries had been established by Sainte Helene at Stavrovouni and Tochni, and by Kalokairos at Saint Nicholas of the Cats. Monasteries were also established in the valleys of Marathasa like that of Saint John Lambadistis which was founded next to St. Heraklidios monastery. The trend for monastic life is connected to the arrival of Saint Hilarion in the island. Together with Saint Anthony, Hilarion had lived for a very long time in the desert. He organised monastic life on the island and his name is connected with the Castle of Saint Hilarion, in the mountains over Kyrenia. He died in 371 A.D.

St. Epiphanius

Saint Epiphanius was a leading personality in the Church of Cyprus. He was Bishop of Salamis - Constantia for 36 years from 368 to 403 A.D. and his authority was so great that Emperor Theodosius ordered the Cypriots to blind obedience of Epiphanius on the pain of exile from the island for any disobedience. He participated in the religious quarrels of his time. He fought Origenis, and on the request of Patriarch of Alexandria Theofilus he convened a synod of all Bishops at Constantia, which condemned the writings of Origenis. He personally carried the synod's findings and verdict to Constantinople. He never returned to Cyprus, however, because he died on his return journey. His body was taken to Constantia where it was buried in the church

A limestone statue of Zeus the "Thunder god". The god held an eagle in his left hand and with the right he was ready to throw his thunderbolt. It was found at Kition, but its Ionic-Hellenic influence is self evident. Around 500 B.C.

The man-like features of this head indicate that he was an athlete. It is a limestone head in natural size and bears a strong influence of Hellenic art. It was found at Potamia and is from the 5th century B.C.

Two copper bracelets of the 5th century B.C. from Kourion. They are gold plated, and terminate in two bulls' heads of an eastern influence.

Golden necklace of the 6th century B.C. from the sanctuary of Golgia Aphrodite at Arsos. In the center it has a pendant with two Egyptian pots with the crowns of upper and Lower Egypt. The short conquest of the island by the Pharaoh Amasis, left vivid and strong traces on the art of the island and particularly in the jeweller´s art.

104

bearing his name. The church of Saint Epiphanius, with it's huge five-aisled basilica was burnt to the ground during the Saracen raids in the seventh century A.D. The ruins of this church were discovered during the excavation of ancient Salamis.

Cyprus as a part of the Eastern Byzantine state   Cyprus remained as part of the Roman Empire until 395 A.D., when Theodosius the Great died and the Roman empire was divided into a Western state with Rome as it's capital, and an Eastern state with Byzantium as its capital. Honorius, son of Theodosius was the emperor in Rome, and Arcadius became the Emperor of Byzantium. Cyprus came under the Eastern Byzantine state and this helped in preserving it's Hellenic character. This also gave rise to the Byzantine period of Cypriot history.

LEARNING AND ARTS UP TO THE BYZANTINE PERIOD

Ionian influence-poetry   There can be no talk of Cypriot literary production before the eighth century B.C., because of lack of both information as well as texts. Recent allegations that the Engomi tablet could be poetry, cannot be substantiated simply because it has not yet been deciphered and thus cannot be read. Things, however, do change after the eighth century B.C., when Cyprus-as already mentioned- developed close ties with the cities of Ionia and Asia Minor. The Homeric epics were widely available in these areas and this made it comparatively easy for the Cypriots to embrace Homeric poetry, and, based upon the contents of the Homeric epics, as well as other traditions and legends, gained through these contacts with the Hellenic world, to create their own poetry.

Stasinus and Cypriot epics   The most ancient poetic work which comes under this influence is the "Cypriot epics" an eleven-volume work dealing with the cause and first years of the Trojan war, up to the point when the Iliad commences. If we are to judge from the few fragments which have so far survived, the work must have been a considerable one and even equal to the Homeric epics, otherwise Homer himself would not have been mentioned as a possible author of the work. It is, however, surmised today that the "Cypriot epics" was the work of the Salaminian poet Stasinus, and that it was written in the seventh century B.C. The variety of myths incorporated in this work, many of which could not have been known to Homer, did inspire the tragedians of ancient Athens into composing their tragedies. «Iphigenia in Aulis», by Euripides, and «Philoctetes» by Sophocles fall within this category.

Egesias and
Euclos

There are a number of other poets, all contemporaries of Stasinus, about whom little is known, but there is mention of Euclos, the epigram writer, who foretold the birth of Homer in Cyprus. Despite the mythical character of this, it demonstrates the degree to which the Homeric epics were known in Cyprus and the very degree to which these epics did influence Cypriot poetry. Egesias of Salamis is another contemporary of the other two and he is mentioned as such by later writers.

Homeric
"Hymns"

The works known as the "Homeric Hymns" were also very well known in Cyprus. Particularly well known, were those which referred to Aphrodite, and which were recited at rites for the goddess in Paphos and at Amathus. An allegation that these hymns could have been the works of Stasinus, or even of Egesias, could certainly stand.

Athenian culture
dominates

For a period after the seventh century B.C. we have no information on Cypriot poets or writers. This, however, must not be considered as either strange or as an explanation that Cypriots could not write. This, rather, was the effect of foreign domination over the island which Evagoras the First, and his successors, attempted to overthrow by making Salamis the center of learning, inviting poets and orators to come to the city from Athens. The names of Isocrates and Andokides are such examples. The cultural presence of Athens in Salamis was so strong that creation of a local cultural life must have been unavoidably overshadowed. This is proved by the fact that although Cypriot literary creators must have existed, such as Ermias the poet, Kleon of Kourion, and the satyric poet Sopatros of Paphos, nothing has been saved from these Ptolemaic times so that we can evaluate their work. The love of the Ptolemies for Greek literature is well established. Their famous library in Alexandria, concentrating the writings of an entire culture and literary production from Greece, is proof of their support and their encouragement of the literary arts. This is also why it becomes certain that in Cyprus also there must have been a flowering of learning, and specifically of dramatic poetry. This is also proved by the preservation of literary names such as those already mentioned, and by the theaters which were built in nearly all the cities of the island. An inscription from the times of the Ptolemies, informs us that a secretariat of actors did exist in the city of Salamis. Writers of fables, as well as historians also flourished during the same period. They are mentioned either by contemporary or later chroniclers and writers. Alexandros of Paphos and Igisandros of Salamis are among fable writers mentioned. Aristos of Salamis and Klearchos of Soloi are mentioned among the historians.

Philosophy   Philosophy itself, however, was developed by the Cypriots in Athens. The first and most prominent philosopher was Zeno of Kition who lived from 336 to 264 B.C. He was the son of a merchant, Mnaseas, who instead of studying commerce when sent to Athens he took up philosophy. In Athens he established his own school of philosophy which greatly influenced Roman philosophy in later years. His philosophy came to be known as stoic because he expounded and taught it in the stoa «Pikili» in Athens. Perseus of Kition was his pupil, and he became prominent as well. Evdimos was another Cypriot philosopher of the Platonic school who studied under Aristotle and became his close friend. Aristotle dedicated one of his works, "Evdimos, or about the soul" to his friend and pupil. We can, in conclusion, also mention Demonax who became prominent in the second century A.D. in Athens. Lucian, who was his contemporary, wrote about Demonax´s life. He was something between a Stoic and a Cynic philosopher and had been greatly influenced by Christianity.

Medicine   Medicine, however, was the field in which the Cypriots excelled. Mention has already been made of Onasilo`s, who was mentioned on the bronze tablet of Idalion as the doctor who gave free treatment to all the wounded in the battle of 460 B.C. Under the Ptolemies many doctors became prominent and their fame spread throughout the Ptolemaic territories. Apollonios of Kition is one of them. He wrote his treaties on joints (Peri Arthron Pragmatia) which has survived to our days, with its 31 illustrations. Another famous doctor was Diagoras who became prominent in the third century and made annotations to the works of Hippocrates. He became prominent through his research on disease of the ear and the eye and discovered a medication for the treatment of ophthalmia. Apollodoros, is another prominent doctor named.

THE ARTS

Oriental influence   As elsewhere, so in Cyprus, the development of styles and forms of art followed historic events. As a result of the island´s position, and because of the commercial transactions and contacts with the East, it was natural for the island to receive influences from Eastern lands. In Cyprus as well as in Greece we have Eastern influences on the arts, mainly during the period from the eighth to the seventh centuries B.C. We find such influences both on pottery, on pottery decoration, as well as in sculpture, architecture and on miniature arts.

Hellenic-Ionic influence   Hellenic influences start from the end of the seventh century B.C., that is the time when Cyprus, free from Assyrian influences, turned towards the Hellenic world and set up close ties, first with the islands, and then with Athens itself. We have already stressed the strong presence of Cycladic pottery in Cyprus. The visit to Aepeia by Athenian statesman Solon was the first contact in such relations which reached their climax in frequency under Evagoras the First. There is no art form which does not verify the live presence of Hellenic art and technique. Pottery and its decoration, sculpture, architecture, miniature arts as well as coin minting were all so influenced by parallel Hellenic trends and primarily Athenian trends, that a student can often wonder whether items were imported or manufactured locally as copies of Hellenic art. The very same trends continued during the Ptolemaic period, and then on into Roman times.

Architecture   Although architectural remains of the Hellenistic and later of the Roman periods are numerous, and more of them are coming to light under archaeological excavation, those of the period between the tenth and seventh centuries B.C., are limited not because no monumental buildings were erected at that time, such as temples and mansions, but rather because new ones were usually built on top of the ruins of older ones, and it is these that the archaeologists are bringing to light. Often, and especially in the case of temples, the new ones follow the architectural arrangement of the old one in such a way that newer buildings look like the older ones.

Temples   The architecture of temples became known to us through a great number of examples. We have examples in the 12th century B.C. Mycenaean temples at Engomi and Kition and the Roman temples of Aphrodite in Paphos and the sanctuary of Apollo Ilates at the city of Kourion. The most elemental form of a sanctuary consisted of an enclosed courtyard, with an altar in the centre., and a tripartite building at one end. We see examples of this both in the temple of Astarte at Kition, as well as of Aphrodite at Paphos. Both these temples were built on the ruins of Mycenaean temples which had been destroyed. This temple arrangement could be the result of an Eastern, or Mycenaean influence. We can see it depicted on coins from Byblos which, on the one side, bear a representation of the temple of Astarte.

The way in which this stylized bird captures the fish, gives an exceptional grace to this wine vessel, executed in the free-field style of the 7th century B.C.

Here, also, the artist depicts the bull, smelling a lotus flower in an exceptional manner. It is known that the bull was a beloved subject in pottery decoration as of very ancient times. 7th century B.C.

The bird is also a very beloved motif for decoration in the free-field of the 7th century B.C. With exceptional artistry, the craftsman here covered the curved surface of the wine vessel with the curved bird, and a tree branch. From Sinda.

On this wine vessel a huge bird gazes at a diminutive man with a comical appearance. It has a rams head, ackward long arms, and the short legs give the impression of terror before the bird. Perhaps here we have another version of the myth on the Mycenaean crater on p. 49. It was found at Arnadhi.

We can also see it in a fresco in the palace of Knossos, in Crete, as well as on the "sanctuaries of the doves," as the five identical golden plaques discovered at Mycenae are named. Temples have been excavated at many ancient sites at Idalion, Soloi, Agia Irene, and at Myrtou-Pigades. This last is of a particular importance, because of the architecture of it´s altar which has been restored. The Hellenic influence on a number of these temples is very important and clear, as in the temple of Athena at Soloi, and Apollo Ilatis at Kourion. These temples had special treasuries for the safe-keeping of gifts, in the manner of the Hellenic temples.

Palaces   Upto this moment, only one palace has been fully excavated. It is the palace of Soloi at Vouni. This, however, is sufficient to illustrate the degree of architectural progress, which carried on the tradition of monumental structures, as we find it in Engomi. This city, itself, as well as it´s buildings, are very surprising for their perfection, which brings to mind modern town-planning principles and views. The Vouni palace is a multi-labyrinthine structure, originally erected at the very beginning of the fifth century B.C., the time when the Persians had suppressed Onesilos´ revolt and gave Soloi to the king of Marion. It is this king of Marion who, in all probability, was the first to build for protection, on top of a hill which is dominating the entire area. The original architectural form of the palace faces East, just like the temples do. When, fifty years later, Kimon liberated Soloi, in 449 B.C., the royal appartments were converted in such a manner that the entire structure took on the form and magnificence of Mycenaean palaces, with the megaron as the central structure and we can see this style of palace at Mycenae, Tiryns, and more recently, and in a better form, at the palace of Nestor at Pylos.

Public buildings   The city of Salamis is a unique archaeological
at Salamis   site in which we can very clearly see buildings for
public use. The most important of these is the complex known as the gymnasium. This one consists of an open air, four sided, arena which is surrounded by colonnades and stoas, surrounded by statues. Many without heads have been excavated. Behind these are the dressing rooms which also had hot-water baths and sweating rooms just as in the palace at Soloi. At Soloi we also find cold-water baths next to the hot-water arrangements. We also find the same arrangements at the Acropolis of Kourion, at the sanctuary of Apollo Ilatis at Kourion, and in the mansions of new Paphos. All these arrangements are surprising because of their excellent construction and functionality of operation. Many frescoes and mosaic floors are to be found in these steam-rooms. They

A general view of the Palace of Soloi, at Vouni, as it developed in the 4th century B.C., with the Mycenaean palace as a model. The grand staircase of the palace is very clearly visible.

The theater of Soloi as it has been rebuilt by the Antiquities Department.

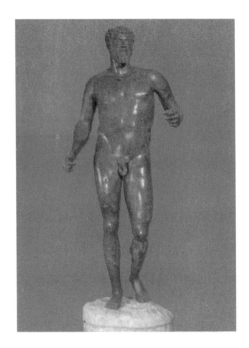

A copper statue of Septimius Severus cast in above-normal size. The statue which depicts the emperor naked, with an athletic body, has all the characteristics of Hellenic-Roman statue manufacture. It was found at Kythrea and is from the 3rd century A.D.

The Eastern colonnade of the gymnasium at Salamis as it was arranged in Roman times.

all depict scenes from Hellenic mythology. The Gymnasium in Salamis also boasted of swimming pools which were supplied with water from a large cistern located at the North end of the agora - another complex of buildings which had been excavated earlier. Water was brought to this cistern by an aqueduct from Kythrea. The stadium was located very near to the gymnasium. Only some tiers of this stadium remain. The theater has already been excavated but the amphitheater, located between the gymnasium and the theater, was not, due to the Turkish invasion. The temple of Salaminian Zeus completed the complex of public building of the city from the Hellenistic, but mainly from Roman times.

Theaters   The intense cultural activity and life of Cyprus is indicated by the theaters. Such theaters were found in all the cities which have been excavated systematically. Nearly all of them were originally built during the Hellenistic period, and they were either reconstructed, or completed during the Roman period. The theater of Salamis is the largest. It was 30 meters high and had 55 tiers of seats with a capacity of fifteen thousand spectators. It's semicircular orchestra has a diameter of 27.50 meters with a stage 40 meters long and 5 meters deep. The proscenium was decorated with statues, pieces, of which were found among the ruins. The theaters at Kourion and Soloi are smaller. They have both been restored and used in our time. The first known odeon has also been discovered recently in Paphos. All these theaters, which were built on the Hellenistic and Roman models, boast of excellent acoustics.

The mansions of   There is an unimaginable wealth and luxury in the
Kourion   mansions of the Hellenistic and Roman times unearthed at Kourion, and more recently in Paphos. The acropolis of Kourion is always of great interest. The discovery of the reception hall for official guests, with its glorious mosaic of Achilles, has added further to this great interest, being of an exceptional composition. It depicts Achilles at the palace of King Lykomedes on Skyros Island, with Ulysses singing his war chant, in his effort to unmask Achilles who is dressed as a maiden. According to the legend, Ulysses managed to do this and led Achilles away despite protestations from Deidamia, daughter of Lykomedes. Near this reception hall, which is situated near today's entrance to the Acropolis, another mansion was discovered with mosaics. These depict gladiators battling wild beasts. More to the South East, there is an old Christian basilica, also with its mosaic floors. Further down, we have the theater, already mentioned, and then the House of Eustolius which boasts of excellent bath installations and beautiful mosaics. This mansion dates from

the latter years of the Roman period, when Christianity had already prevailed in the island.

More mansions in Paphos   The mansions discovered in New Paphos are far wealthier and more luxurious. As we know the Ptolemies had transferred their capital to this city, and this brought about a fast development and a high level of civilization. This is demonstrated in the house of Dionysos and in another, with its mosaic of the Labyrinth. The House of Dionysos is an extremely complex structure, with bedrooms, baths, a fish pond, all surrounded by colonnades, with kitchens and workshops. What makes this mansion unique are its multi-coloured mosaics, all of an excellent composition with a startling severity of form which are serene, but also with a violence of movement, and complex borders. Hunting and other scenes, taken from Hellenic mythology, with Dionysos predominant, give the floors a fantastic character. Here we have Pyramus and Thisbe, further on there is Dionysos himself. We have Icarios and Neptune with Amymone, with Apollo and Daphne not far away. The culmination is in the Triumph of Dionysos sitting on a chariot drawn by panthers. As it survives, this building dates from Roman times, but it is built on top of a Hellenistic building as proved by a treasure of some 2,400 silver four-drachma coins of the third to the first century B.C., which were discovered under one of the Roman mosaics. The rooms of this mansion were also decorated by wall paintings making this mansion unique for its time. Unfortunately very little of these has remained. There is another, even larger mansion which, if we are to judge from its painted walls and mosaics already discovered, must have been even more luxurious than the House of Dionysos. The excavations of this mansion are still continuing. The most beautiful of the mosaics is the composition of the Labyrinth. In the centre of this circular composition we have Theseus. On his right there is Crete personified and on his left we have Ariadne. The Minotaur is at his feet, and Theseus is ready to strike him with his sword. Another mosaic depicts the birth of Achilles. Thetis and Peleus are on a throne with the fates, Clotho, Atropos, and Lachesis behind them. A nurse holds Achilles on her knees just before immersing him into the bath of immortality. Apart from their innate beauty, these two excellent mosaics, together with those of the House of Dionysos, demonstrate clearly that Hellenic mythology subjects were extremely popular in ancient Cyprus.

The tombs   We close the chapter on architecture with a reference to the tombs, of the period under examination. With the exception of the grand royal tombs of Salamis which date

This mosaic is situated in the second mansion of Paphos, and shows Theseus killing the Minotaur. The Labyrinth and Crete have been personified. The whole composition makes this mosaic one of the most beautiful finds from the 3rd century A.D.

This mosaic from Paphos is incomparable in beauty, composition, imagination and colour. It is situated in the House of Dionysos and relates the tradition about the cultivation of the vine by Icarios. A crowned and seated Dionysos on the left, has Acme half lying in front of him. The god is offering a bunch of grapes, while Icarios leading an ox cart laden with wine skins stretches his hand to receive it from him. Behind the cart, the drunken shepherds who were the first to taste Icarios' wine. As we know from mythology they killed him in their drunkenness, believing that he had poisoned them.

from the eighth to the seventh centuries B.C., as well as certain others with which we will deal separately, the rest of the tombs follow the local tradition which prevailed since the Copper era. As a rule, a lengthy corridor leads to the mouth of the chamber which is dug out of the rock, or earth, and in which the dead were placed. There were always numerous offerings of items of daily use, personal adornments and jewellery, as well as weapons. Religious items, such as small idols were also present. The entrance to the burial chamber was sealed with a stone slab. Funeral rites were performed in the corridor after burial, and also, perhaps, at specified times of the year. These included libations as well as the sacrifice of animals. These funerary rites, as well as the architecture of chamber tombs, were common both in the East, as well as in the Aegean areas. Cremation of the dead, however, which was common practice in Crete and in the Hellenic world, is not met in Cypriot rites before the Archaic era.

The royal tombs of Salamis   The architectural arrangement of the Royal Tombs of Salamis is approximately the same but it has a very basic difference. The corridor and the chambers are not dug out of the rock or the earth . They are both built of hewn stones which give the tombs their royal magnificence. The corridors are particularly grand. Their purpose was not simply to lead to the burial chamber. They were primarily used for the funerary rites and ceremonies. Numerous offerings have been discovered on the floor of corridors. The most impressive find, however, was the discovery of the skeletons of horses, and the remnants of some chariots. In one instance, the skeletons of two horses were found just as they had been sacrificed, their collars attached to the chariot´s yoke, with the metal attachments and the horses golden ornaments on the floor. In another grave, and in addition to the chariots and a great number of copper pieces of horse equipment, there were also two royal thrones and a couch decorated with ivory inlay work and placed in such a manner as to respond to Homer´s description of similar items placed in graves. Also in the same corridors was a large copper cauldron decorated with plastically rendered griffins and sirens along its rim. There are nine in all such Royal Tombs, one of which has become known as the prison of Sainte Catherine, which is situated near the Monastery of Saint Barnabas. Another grave which does not consist of a chamber and corridor, but which was simply a platform covered by a mound of earth, has been interpreted as a cenotath for the last of the Teucridae, Nicocreon and his family, who had committed suicide, in order to avoid becoming the prisoners of Ptolemy the First. The volume and the quality of funerary offerings found in these graves has justified their classification and description as Royal Tombs. The many golden and copper wreaths, iron javelins, alabaster pots and, mainly, the portraits of four men and one woman found in the cenotaph, are interpreted as a monument erected by the people of Salamis to honour the family of the last Teucrid.

Other Royal tombs   Royal tombs with the same magnificent appearance, have been also discovered in other parts of Cyprus. The most important are the Royal Tombs of Amathus, of Tamassos (present-day Politico), of Pyla and primarily of New Paphos. The ones in Paphos, known as tombs of the kings, are hewn out of solid rock with burial niches situated around a collonaded courtyard in the Doric style. The friezes, cornices, and other architectural decorations, give the entire structure the aspect of monumental architucture of the type one meets in Alexandrian burial grounds. This could justify the view that these tombs could be the tombs of Ptolemaic nobles.

Ceramics   Objects manufactured from clay, will be divided into two categories: clay pottery and clay idols. As we already know, Cyprus is a country in which pottery-making was a special industry right from the beginning of the copper era. It´s products were exported to all neighbouring countries. The craftsmen of the island had an unlimited imagination. This allowed them to combine the various foreign elements to which they were exposed through contacts with other people and their art. They made original pottery in a variety of shapes and diversity in the decorative motifs. They maintained this ability of theirs through the historic era. During the few centuries of this era, in which the geometric style was developed, from the 11th to the eighth century B.C., Cypriot pottery combined the local with the Mycenaean tradition, creating the Cypro-Mycenaean art which has bequeathed to us some of the most beautiful pottery which today adorns the Cyprus Archaeological Museum. Eastern influences began to appear with the seventh century B.C., and the Cypriot potters began to absorb the Eastern influences for a very long time, but without rejecting the Hellenic influences which, by the sixth century B.C., percolated throughout the whole island.

Pottery and it´s decoration   Influences are evidently stronger in the decoration of pottery rather than in shapes. On a very beautiful amphora from the end of the eighth century B.C., which bears the name of Hubbard - it´s donor - we see a decorative style with an interwoven Hellenic and an Eastern influence. Perhaps this is the first rather timid attempt by a Cypriot potter to imitate Eastern

A royal throne, which with two others and a couch , were found in a royal tomb at Salamis. It was entirely covered with ivory of which one piece depicts a Sphinx, as seen in the picture below. Dr. Vassos Karageorgis observed that this throne brings to mind the royal thrones mentioned in Mycenaean tablets from Pylos, and particularly the one of Penelope as described by Homer in the Odyssey. 8th century B.C.

The ivory plague, with a sphinx and a second one with a lotus flower on it, were set between the seat and the arms of the throne.

Left: A copper cauldron resting on a tripod found in a Salamis royal tomb of the 8th century B.C. Eight griffins in relief and four double-faced sirens around the rim give the cauldron an exceptional splendour.

Right: A silver studded sword from a Salamis royal tomb which is extremely close to Homer´s description of the swords of the Achaeans. End of the 8th century B.C.

motifs. Potters later became much bolder and the entire seventh century B.C., is dominated by this Eastern influence. Certain oenohoe, or wine vessels, decorated in a free painted style, have birds as their dominant feature, with some interwoven lotus flowers executed in very beautiful colour combinations. These demonstrate the artistry of the Cypriot potters, which has survived into our own times. After the sixth century B.C., the close ties between Cyprus and Hellenic Greece, introduced a very strong Hellenic influence upon Cypriot pottery and it´s decoration. There is such a dearth of red and black Attic pottery found in graves of the classical period, that they could not leave Cypriot potters without their influence. This influence continued through the Hellenistic periods, during which not only pottery and it´s decoration, but also every other form of art became purely Hellenistic in style thanks to the influence of the Ptolemies. During the Roman period, pottery began to lose it´s old grandeur, because the use of glass became more prevalent.

Clay idols   Clay idols form the second branch of ceramic art. Their making started with the Chalcolithic era and continued right through the copper era, without diminishing, and it reached it´s climax primarily after the eighth century B.C. There is no rural site in Cyprus which was either excavated, or simply identified as a place of worship, which was not full of such idols, donated as offerings to the dead. Human figurines, masked priests, centaurs, dancers and musicians with cymbals, singers, warriors either on foot or astride horses, chariots, all of these go to make up the most usual types of these idols. Among these offerings we even find replicas of ships with oarsmen, as well as various compositions depicting the daily life of these people. A good example of this is found in a composition discovered in an archaic place of worship, which depicts a woman in birth helped by a midwife. This was discovered in a Lapithos area grave. There are other examples discovered at other sites which depict the grinding of wheat and other domestic activities. The idols of the seventh century B.C., demonstrate a strong Eastern influence. From the sixth century, however, we have the emergence of a strong Hellenic influence, mostly of an Ionic origin. Hellenic influence reached the climax of faithful copying, from the sixth century B.C., onwards, with the Tanagra maiden as the most prominent example. A very great number of these maidens were discovered in Cypriot graves and elsewhere.

Sculpture   Progress in sculpture is, evidently, similar to progress in pottery. At first, we have Eastern influences with obvious elements from Egyptian art. Later, in the sixth century

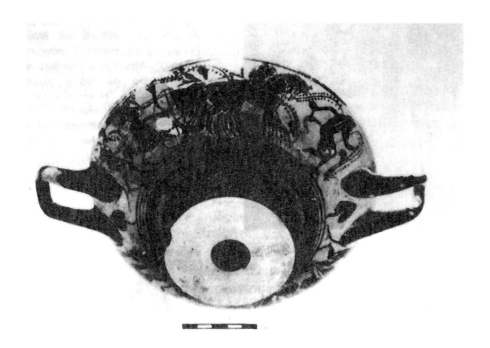

A very great number of Attic pots, both black as well as red figure, were found in Cypriot graves of the 6th and 5th centuries B.C. They were so beautiful both in shape as well as in decoration, that wealthy Cypriots preferred them to Cypriot pottery. We present a number of such pots in the next pages. Here we have a black decorated cup from Marion of the late 6th century B.C. The decoration is Dionysian on both sides, made up of a chariot with four horses with maenads and satyrs in a frenzied dance.

A relief votive offering of excellent technique, made of Paros marble which was found at Mersinaki, near Soloi. The goddess, either Athena or Artemis, wears a veil and a cloak over her shoulders. The influence of classical Greek art is self evident. It was in all probability imported from some island. 5th cent. B.C.

A clay figurine in the Tanagraia style from a grave at Soloi. In its right hand it is holding a bunch of grapes while with the other it is coquetishly lifting its pleated tunic. 4th cent. B.C.

B.C., we have Ionic influences and later, we have Hellenic influence from the classic up to the Roman times. Statues are, usually sculpted out of sand stone but a number are also sculpted from marble. Some marble heads from Arsos and Soloi are excellent examples of Hellenic art with a Cypriot tint, like the ones found at Salamis, Kition, Kourion, New Paphos and at Marion. At Marion we have grave stones which are very worthy of note. One, from the fifth century B.C., apart from being sculpted in an excellent Hellenic style, also has a great historic value, because it demonstrates how Evagoras the First influenced the whole island culturally. The stele is dedicated to a Salaminian maiden. The inscription, written in the Cypriot syllabic script, states: I am Aristilia, daughter of Onasilos, from Salamis.

Metal work ancient times
Metal working by the Cypriots dates to very ancient times. Copper statuettes found in temples at Engomi and Kition demonstrate a very advanced technique. A great number of them have been found, and they depict gods, but mostly the protector of mines, who has been identified as Keraiatis Apollo. The same advanced technique is found in the case of certain tripods, the statues of bulls, in ceremonial compositions, all of them dating from the 12th century B.C. This tradition has been followed without a break through to the Hellenic era, giving us works of art of an incomparable artistry as well as technique. A copper bull, as well as the composition of two lions savaging a bull, found at Soloi, are works of high artistic inspiration, in which the Hellenic influence is self-evident. A multitude of copper art decorating show cases in the Cyprus and many foreign museums, all demonstrate this high level of technique developed by the Cypriot metal worker. The statue of Septimius Severus demonstrates that this level did not drop with the passage of time, but that rather the contrary happened. It reached the point when monumental works of art like this statue were made even down into Roman times.

Gold and silver ware
The working of gold and silver in Cyprus also goes back to very ancient times. Gold and silver jewellery of very high craftsmanship and art have been found in the Mycenaean graves of Engomi and Kition dating to the 14th century B.C. Necklaces, rings, as well as earrings and metal bands, all of a very high degree of craftmanship, together with a royal scepter of gold and enamel, all these go to testify to the wealth amassed in Cyprus as a result of the commerce conducted. All these objects also give an example of the good taste cultivated by the inhabitants. All this was continued through to the historic era. The ordinary as well as the royal tombs of

Salamis, the ruins of New Paphos, of Marion as well as Soloi, have given us excellent examples of this continued art of working in gold and silver, and of the wealth and good taste which existed in Cyprus. This is also supported by numberless items in ivory, such as mirror handles, and ivory inlays on thrones, such as those of Salamis.

Miniatures and coins Cylinders, ring stones and scarabs are works of miniature art which, together with the coins, complete the examples of Cypriot art. In his miniature art the Cypriot craftsman did not rise to the heights of the Egyptians and other Eastern peoples, or the imagination of the Minoans and the Mycenaean craftsmen. Preserved examples of such Cypriot miniature art, however, give us a delicate and true description of the subject copied in miniature art. In conclusion, the privilege of Cypriot kings to mint their own coins, led to the minting of a great variety of coins on the island. The main characteristic of most of them, specially those minted by Evagoras the First and his successors in Salamis, is their pure Hellenic character, with the images of gods and of heroes on their faces. During Hellenistic times, the Ptolemies kept the privilege for themselves, and they minted coins with their own image on one side. The same practice was followed by the Roman emperors during the Roman era.

Votive offerings of images of warriors, like the shield bearer, here, are very common in sanctuaries, as we can also see in the Agia Irene small statuettes. 6th cent. B.C.

Images of daily life are also to be found in graves and sanctuaries. Here one woman feeds grain from a trough into the grinder, which is turned by another woman seated opposite. 6th century B.C. from Tamassos.

A black-figure attic cup of the 6th century B.C. Alternating figures of naked hoplites and riders make up the decoration.

The way in which the two lions are tearing into the cow on this black figure attic cup from Marion, recalls to mind the copper composition from Soloi, which we shall see elsewhere.

A black-figure Attic peliki of the 6th century B.C. with on both sides Theseus
slaying the Minotaur.

A black-figure Attic amphora from
Tamassos. 540-530 B.C.

A red-figure Attic lykithos. A bearded and long haired dancer, perhaps Dyonysos himself, dances with arms akimbo, and his head turned to the right. 480-460 B.C.

A black-figure Attic bowl of the end of the 6th century B.C. Two figures on either side of a chariot with four horses gaze at it while two sphinxes are perched at the end of the scene with their backs to each other.

130

Marion has given us some of the most beautiful grave
stones with a strong Hellenic influence. The naked
youth stands before a stele with his cloak over the left
shoulder. His graceful stance recalls an Attic technique. 5th century B.C.

Another example of Ionic influence, this time in the terracotta of a kore. The votive tomb statue with its characteristic Ionian smile gives the impression of deep sorrow. 6th to the 5th century B.C.

A clay composition of an Eros seated on a ram. The potter gave life to the joy and enthusiasm of the winged god in an exemplary manner. The god obviously enjoys his ride on the galopping ram. Greco-Roman period.

A statue of Aphrodite from Soloi with all the characteristics of sculpture
from the Hellenistic period. 1st cent. B.C.

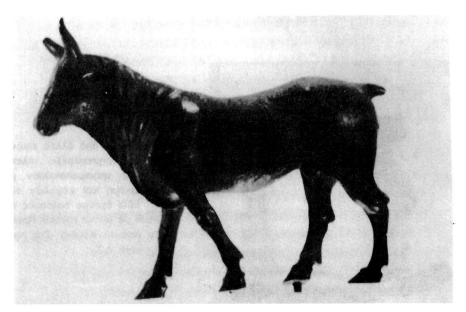

A copper statue of a cow from Soloi. The rendering is so realistic and fine that its maker must have been a student of Myron´s school of sculptures. 5th century B.C.

The rendering of two lions tearing apart a struggling cow, is something more than alive. The copper composition was found in company with the copper cow above in the same sanctuary of Athena at Soloi.

We know from other sources that in religious ceremonies the priests used to don bull-head masks. Here we have statuettes of two figures wearing bullhead masks. It was found at Kourion. 6th century B.C.

An idol of the Tanagra type, of an actor wearing a mask. He is wearing a rich, pleated Chiton and also wears a cloak over his shoulder. He is wearing buskins on his feet. Found in a Soloi grave of the 4th century B.C.

136

A general view of the sanctuary of Apollo Ilatis at Kourion.

A mosaic floor from the House of Dionysos. The theme is the myth of Thisbe and Pyramos, as described by Ovid. On the left Thisbe is fleeing in terror from an attacking lioness in the centre, holding a piece of Thisbe´s torn dress. On the right Pyramos is on the ground with a cornucopia in hand.

Another mosaic from the House of Dionysos. This time the theme is the myth of Apollo and Daphne. Before Apollo we have the bush of Daphne (laurel) which is to take the place of the nymph, and from which the god will break a branch to make his wreath. Ever since laurel has remained the symbol of the crowning of victors in all noble contests.

THE BYZANTINE PERIOD

THE AUTOCEPHALUS CHURCH OF CYPRUS

The Partiarchs of Antiocheia   Under Emperor Constantine the Great, Cyprus was administratively placed under the Eastern Administration with Antiochia as the capital. The patriarchs of Antiochia demanded that the church of Cyprus should also come under them. They based their demand on that the consularius, or governor of Cyprus, was appointed by the Count of Antiochia, as well as on a forged canon of the First Ecumenical Synod of Nicaea which stated that the patriarch of Antiochia had the right to nominate the archbishop of Cyprus.

Third Ecumenical Synod of Ephesus   The Antiochia's demands were presented to Pope Innocent the first by Patriarch Alexander who was only attempting to strengthen his own personal position. The Bishops of Cyprus, however, defied an order from the Pope to comply. They repeated their refusal in 431 A.D., when they ingored instructions from the Count of Antiochia Flavius Dionysus and elected Reginus to replace the bishop of Constantia Theodoros, and thus rejected any intervention from the Patriarch of Antiochia. On his election, Reginus, accompanied by three other Bishops proceeded to Ephesus where the third Ecumenical Synod was meeting, and managed to gain approval of the famous Eighth Canon of Ephesus, which gave recognition to the autocephalus character of the Church of Cyprus.

Anthemios and the remains of Barnabas   Even after this ruling, however, those in Antiochia, acting on the basis of some vague wording of the Eighth canon, continued to promote their demands. While this was going on, Bishop Anthemios of Constantia saw a vision of Saint Barnabas, who pointed out to him the place of his burial. He found the place, with the saint's remains and the hand-written Gospel by Matthew on his chest, as it was placed there by Mark the Evangelist. This discovery left no doubt that the Church of Cyprus was indeed an Apostolic Church and that as such, it had every right to be recognised as autocephalus.

Final Recognition and privileges   Following his discovery, Anthemios went to Constantinople, taking the saint's remains and the Gospel with him. He requested that Emperor Zenon should put an end to the dispute with Antioch. Zenon called a special session of the synod in Constantinople in 488 A.D., which, without any shadow of a doubt, ratified the Eighth Canon of Ephesus, closing the affair once and for all. Before leaving Constantinople, Anthemios presented the Gospel to the Emperor and it was placed within the chapel of Saint Stephen, which was in the Royal Palace, with instructions that it should be read from during the Easter Services. In an expression of gratitude to Anthemios the Emperor granted the following privileges to Anthemios and his successors: a - to sign in red ink like the emperors; b - to carry a royal scepter instead of the customary Pastoral Staff; and c - to wear a red cloak. These privileges are enjoyed to this day by the archbishops of Cyprus.

The Penthekti Ecumenical Synod   Two centuries later, the Cypriots were forced to abandon the island because of incessant raids. On the recommendation of Emperor Justinian the Second, they settled on the Hellespont near Kyzicos, where they built Justinianopolis and made it the Seat of Archbishop Ioannis. However, there had to be a new ratification of the eighth canon of Ephesus if the archbishop was to maintain the autocephalus character of the church. This was done under the 39th Canon of the Penthekti Synod at Troullos of Constantinople, in 692 A.D. When the Cypriots returned to the island, they built Nea Justiniani, on the ruins of Constantia, which had been sacked. From that time on the Archbishop fo Cyprus also bears the title of Archbishop of Nea Justiniani and of the Whole of Cyprus.

SARACEN RAIDS

Justinian's interest   After the Kalokairos revolt, Cyprus lived in peace for some two centuries. Once again it prospered thanks to the personal interest of the Byzantine emperors. It is on record that Justinian the Great built the «poor-house of Agios Konon» and also repaired the aqueduct which carried water from Kythrea to Salamis, or Constantia. The same emperor also introduced silk worm cultivation to the island, and thus made production of silk one of the island's most flourishing industries. The very same interest was continued by Emperor Heraklios.

Abu Bekr a   New misfortunes befell the island as a result of
possible raid   raids by Saracens which went on for nearly three
centuries. During this period Cyprus was truly ravaged and destroyed. The people, as we already saw, had to leave it seeking shelter elsewhere. The first, possible, such raid is mentioned in 632 A.D., when Abu Bekr, the father in law of Prophet Mohammed plundered the island in a raid of piracy. According to one legend, his daughter fell from her horse and was killed during the siege of Kition. In honour of her memory he built a mosque on the spot where she was buried, known as the Hala Sultan Tekke on the shores of Larnaca Salt Lake. The most likely version of the legend, however, is that the incident rather refers to the wife of Muawiyah, Umm Haram, because it is established by records that he did raid the island in 647 A.D.

The Muawiyah **raid**   Muawiyah, who was the Emir of Syria, raided the
island with a fleet of 700 ships. With this powerful armada he captured Constantia ransacking it of all treasure, and put the inhabitants to the sword. Without any resistence, he managed to capture the entire island and imposed an annual tax of 7,200 gold coins on the people. Six years later, in 653 A.D. he once again raided the island and, after ransacking Constantia once more, he marched on Lapithos which he captured and destroyed. On leaving the island he left behind an army of 12 thousand men. This time the destruction of Constantia was so thourough and great, that the city was completely abandoned. The inhabitants and the See of the Archbishop were taken to neighbouring Arsinoe which had been built by Ptolemy Philadelphus.

Cypriots leave   In 690 A.D. Emperor Justinian the Second saw
that a new attack on the island was very likely and advised Archbishop Ioannis to leave the island together with his flock to go to a safe country until the danger was gone. As we have seen they emigrated to the Hellespont, and settled near Kyzikos. They remained there for eight years. Many perished on the journey, while many others decided to settle in Asia Minor and in Syria. The repatriation of those who remained took place in 698 A.D. under the initiative of the new Byzantine Emperor Tiberius the Third. This transfer of the population was considered an act of madness because the island's population decreased considerably as a result.

Raids by Walid and by Harun al Rashid   Saracen raids against the island were repeated in 744 A.D. under Walid the 2nd, and again in 806 A.D. under Caliph Harun al Rashid who, after ransacking the island from one end to the other, burnt all the churches. He also took with him sixteen thousand prisoners whom he sold as slaves in Syria. The Archbishop was one of them.

Cyprus as subject of the Byzantine Empire   Nearly an entire century passed without new mention of Saracen raids of any large scale. This was a sufficiently long interval to permit the recuperation of Cyprus from past scars. This was also aided by administrative changes implemented by Emperor Basil the First of Macedon, 867-886 A.D., who proclaimed Cyprus a subject of the empire and appointed General Alexios as governor of the island. He did administer the island in a just and fatherly manner for seven years, and his policy was pursued by his successors who took a special care of Cyprus.

Nikiforos Fokas - An end to the raids   New raids are recorded in 904 and 911 A.D., even though information is rather sketchy. It is evident that until 965 A.D., the Saracens did have a control over the island but things began to change from 960 A.D. when Emperor Romanos the Second put into effect the so-called extermination war assisted by General Nikiforos Fokas. In an effort to put an end to the situation in Cyprus, once and for all. Nikiforos Fokas captured Crete and focused his attention on the Arabs in Asia Minor. He fought them, even after he became Emperor of Byzantium in 963 A.D., and their defeat and the cleansing of Asia Minor was completed by 965 A.D. It was then, when after defeating the Saracen fleet off the Asia Minor shore, when he landed in Cyprus, liberating the island from Saracen influence once and for all. This put an end to the island's lengthy tragedy under the Saracens, the decimation of its population and to the destruction of grand monuments which testified to the island's lengthy grandeur and heritage.

National spirit   It is argued that because of the lengthy raids which went on for three whole centuries, and which annihilated a great part of the population, but also because the island was detached from Byzantium for a number of periods, Cyprus lost its Hellenic character. This however, is nothing but a distortion of historic fact. It is certain that in no instance did these raids take the form of colonization by the Saracens, which could affect and alter the ethnologic composition of the island's population. The Arab-Saracens were nothing more than raiders and pirates. Their only interest was to plunder, capture slaves and gather wealth. In these endeavours, they left only ruin behind them and they also decimated the population. The survivors of these raids kept their ethnic spirit and national feelings very strong. The numberless Byzantine churches with which they replaced those destroyed and lost, the superb frescoes and icons with which they decorated them, and most of all the heroic epics and poems with which they immortalised the tragic events at the end of these raids, all these demonstrate that the trials and suffering during the raids only went to strengthen, and not to sap, the national and ethnic feelings of the people. At the same time, the fact that because of weakness and because they had to protect the main part of the empire, does not mean that the Byzantine Emperors abandoned the island and did not want to protect it. They never stopped considering Cyprus as part of the Hellenic Byzantine world and as a part of their empire. The last operation of Nikiforos Fokas in the island of Crete, as well as in Asia Minor and Cyprus, on the contrary , proves beyond any shadow of a doubt the intent of the Byzantine emperors to keep and protect the part of their Empire to which Cyprus belonged naturally.

REVOLTS BY GOVERNORS

Theofilos Erotikos Cyprus hardly had time to recover from the
1042 A.D. raids, when new calamities befell on it, this time
coming from the part of administrators, commanders and governors who aspired to become independent grandies. The first such revolt took place in 1042 A.D., and was led by Theofilos Erotikos who was appointed the island's administrator by Emperor Michael the Fourth, two years earlier. After Michael's death and his succession by Empress Zoe, Theofilos incited the Cypriots to revolt and placed himself at the head of this act against the throne. The revolt, however, was suppressed by Zoe's successor, Constantine the Gladiator one year later.

Rapsomatis revolt The revolt by Rapsomatis in 1092 was more seri-
1092 A.D. ous. It broke out at the same time as other revolts in
different parts of the Empire, in Crete and on the islands. Alexios Comnenos, Emperor at the time, sent Ioannis Dukas to restore order. He first suppressed the revolt on the other islands, and then he attacked Cyprus and managed to capture Kerynia in a surprise attack. Rapsomatis, who had massed his forces in Nicosia, hastily fortified the pass at Boghaz in his effort to stop Dukas' advance under the command of general Emmanouil Voutomitis. Many of Rapsomatis' forces de-

serted to Voutomitis and this forced the renegade administrator to flee in haste to Limassol from where he hoped to escape. Voutomitis, however, gave chase and forced Rapsomatis to take shelter at the Monastery of Stavrovouni, where he was captured.

Fortification of Cyprus

The times when these developments were taking place were extremely critical for the Byzantine Empire because of the Crusades, with which they coincided. Thus the island became very essential to the Byzantine Emperors for obvious and very strategic reasons. Alexios Comnenos resolved to fortify the island and built the castles of Saint Hilarion, Buffavento, and Kantara on the Pendadaktylos range. He appointed commanders of these castles who he could trust implicitly.

Kykko Monastery

The founding of Kykko Monastery is related to Emmanouil Voutomitis, According to the chronicle, Voutomitis contracted an incurable desease from which, however, he was cured by a monk called Isaias who lived in caves in the Kykko mountains. Voutomitis, as a gift convinced the emperor to make a present to Isaias of an icon of the Virgin Mary painted by Saint Luke, which had been kept in the emperor's palace. The emperor was also convinced to build the monastery paying for it out of empire funds. He also supplied the monastery with goods and granted it benefits. Since that time the monastery earned for itself great fame throughout the whole of Christendom because of miracles which were performed by the Virgin Mary. Apart from other damage sustained by it, the monastery was also destroyed by fire four times, in 1365, 1542, 1751 and in 1813. It remains the primary monastery on the island.

The first Crusades

The island did not escape unscathed from the crusades. Right from the First Crusade its shores were plundered by crusaders who, however, were defeated by Commander Filokalis when they attempted a large scale landing in 1099 A.D. Another operation by Prince Renaldo of Antioch, however, in 1155 A.D., did not have the same fate. Under the excuse that the emperor had reneged on some promise, the prince attacked and captured the island. He also took prisoner both Dukas and Ioannis Comnenos, a nephew of Emperor Manuel Comnenos. Chroniclers record that the prince not only plundered the island, but also committed crimes against both the clergy and the people at large. In 1159 A.D. he was forced to abandon the island because he could not face the emperor's forces sent against him.

Venetian privileges   In addition to raids and foreys during the crusades, the island was also subjected to a peaceful penetration. This was the arrival and settlement on the island of a large number of Venetian merchants in the various towns. Emperor Manuel Comnenos granted them a great number of commercial privilages, in 1148 A.D.

Conquest by Isaakios Komnenos   In 1180 A.D. Emperor Manuel Comnenos appointed his nephew Isaac Dukas Comnenos as Governor of Cilicia. He was taken captive by the Armenians who sold him as a slave to the Knights Templars. He was ransomed and freed by Manuel's successor, Andronikos the First, Comnenos, with guarantees from his friends Constantine Makrodukas and Andronikos Dukas in 1184 A.D. Being a trouble maker by nature, he put together an amy and a fleet and one year later he landed in Cyprus. He used forged papers and credentials to convince the local authorities that he had been appointed the island's administrator by the emperor, and took over authority without any bloodshed.

King Isaakios'   On hearing the news, Emperor Andronikos executed Isaakios' two guarantors and prepared to campaign against him. He was, however, overthrown by the people and was succeeded by Isaakios the Angel. Because of the island's strategic importance to the empire, and because it was being threatened by two strong enemies, and aspiring conquerors, the Turks which were emerging on the world stage, and by the crusaders, the plans of Andronikos against Isaakios were put into effect by the new Emperor. He sent a strong army and fleet against Isaakios under Admiral Ioannis Kontostefanos and General Alexios Comnenos in 1186 A.D. Isaakios then formed an alliance with the King of Sicily William the Second, and with his help he defeated the imperial forces and remained master of the situation. He declared himself king, and ruled with his such harshness that the Cypriots wanted to get rid of him the soonest possible. This occurred five years later, but not in the way in which the Cypriots wanted. Isaakios' overthrow was connected with the final subjugation of the island to foreigners.

Richard the Lionheart   The conquest of Jerusalem by Saladin in 1187 A.D., led to the Third Crusade under Philip Augustus of France, and Richard the Lionheart of England. While sailing from Messina to the Holy Land, the Lionheart came up against a storm and his ships were scattered. Three of them sought refuge in Limassol. Two of them were wrecked and only one managed to reach port. On board were Berengaria, Princess and daughter of the King of Navarre, to whom Richard was betrothed while wintering in Messina. She was accompanied by Joanna of Sicily, the Lionheart's own sister. Isaakios did collect the shipwrecked company, but not in order to help. Having personally suffered in the hands of the Crusaders, he hated all Latins to such a degree that he had formed an alliance with Saladin and pledged not to allow any Crusader ships to resupply on the island. The attempt of Isaakios Comnenos to capture Berengaria and Joanna, however, failed. Lionheart had collected his fleet and landed in Limassol. His landing was without any trouble, and Isaakios was forced to withdraw to Kilani with his forces in 1191 A.D. It is certain that the Lionheart did not plan to capture Cyprus. He sought a meeting with Isaakios in order to solve their differences. This took place in Limassol and it was agreed that Richard would leave Cyprus while Isaakios would stop operations against the Latins allowing the resupply of their ships, and help the Third Crusade by offering 200 men. Isaakios reneged on the agreement and the two armies clashed at Kolossi where Richard won, forcing the Cyprus army to withdraw to Nicosia. Richard returned to Limassol where he married Berengaria in Saint George's chapel. He also formed an alliance with Guy de Luzignan, king of Jerusalem, and went after Isaakios who collected his army in the Mesaoria plain. The clash of the two armies took place near Trimithounda and Richard was victorious. He easily captured all the forts and became master of the whole island. Isaakios himself was taken prisoner. This capture of Cyprus was an important development for the crusaders who lost all their conquests in the Holy Land. In this way they could now use the island as a supply base for their operations.

Representative governors   Enforcing Frankish laws Richard took from the inhabitants half their land in property and holdings, which he divided among his officers as fiefdoms. He then replaced the local garrisons with his own troops in the cities and the castles and he appointed Richard Cambil and Robert Turnham as local governors and as his representatives. The Lionheart then left for Syria to join the other crusaders, taking Isaakios in chains, with him. He handed Isaakios over to the Knights Templars who locked him up in the Castle of Marcada near Tripoli. He died there in 1195 A.D. Thus ended the life of the man who became the reason for Cyprus falling into the hands of the Franks.

Richard and the Templars   On Richard's departure, the Cypriots rose up against the harsh Frankish yoke in a revolt which, however, Turnham suppressed with ease. This revolt, however, worried

Richard who did not intend to detach any forces in order to strengthen the island's garrison. In an effort to get rid of this problem he sought a buyer for the island. The Knights Templars undertook to pay Richard an advance of 40 thousand gold Byzants and another 60 thousand in installments.

Nicosia revolt
Guy de Luzignan

The Templars, a religious order formed in 1181, who joined the crusades, were only interested in enriching their own coffers. To achieve this, they pillaged the island and enforced very heavy taxes. This forced the people of Nicosia to revolt forcing the 117 Knights to lock themselves up in the city's fort. On Easter Sunday, April 6, 1192 the Knights armed themselves and charged out of the fort wanting to die as knights. The local garrison and rebels were caught napping and the knights massacred them. This massacre was extended to surrounding villages, forcing a great number of people to seek refuge in the mountains. Like Richard, however, the knights realised they could not hold onto the island, and they sold it to Guy de Luzignan who had formed an alliance with Richard. The conditions of sale were the same as those of the knights and Richard. When the island was handed over in 1192 A.D., this formed the Frankish domination of the island.

ARTS AND LEARNING UNDER THE BYZANTINE EMPIRE

Leontios Bishop
of Neapolis

Like the Greeks in other parts of the Hellenic world, the Cypriots also devoted themselves to writing books on religious and church matters throughout the Byzantine era. The presence of Cypriot bishops in the various Holy Synods and their handling of dogma, demonstrates the depth of their scholarship in the Holy Scriptures. Leontios Bishop of Neapolis, now Limassol, became very prominent in the fifth century under Emperor Mavrikios. The Seventh Ecumenical Synod which met in Nicaea in 787 A.D. to settle the conflict over the return of icons to the churches, heard a treatise by Leontios on the matter. Leontios had also whitten on the lives of Patriarch Ioannis of Alexandria and Saint Symeon and Spiridon.

Saint Epiphanios

Prominent church writers had existed even before Leontios. Bishop Philon of the Karpass wrote a memorandum on the Song of Songs which still survives. Bishops Theodoros of Chytri wrote on the life of Saint John the Baptist and Epiphanios Bishop of Constantia wrote on science and theology.

Saint Neophytos   Saint Neophytos was another very prominent personality in the Church of Cyprus. Born in Lefkara in 1134 A.D., he was educated at Saint Chrysostomos Monastery which he joined at 18. After much roaming he ended in Paphos near which he built his Engleistra or isolation cell. He lived there to the end of his life with his pupils, painting and writing. His best known treatise is a record of calamities brought to Cyprus by Isaakios Comnenos and the resulting intervention by foreigners. He also wrote sixteen theological works.

Hymn writers   Saint Epiphanio, Philon and Saint Neophytos, already mentioned, were among Cypriot hymn writers. Many others are unknown but they have written and composed services for the saints, like the one for Saints Riginos and Orestes, the services for Saint Heraklidios and Saint John Lambadistis, which are preserved in the Church of Saint Lazaros in Larnaca.

Heroic Epics   During the Saracen and Arab raids, the Byzan-
and songs   tine emperors appointed their bravest soldiers as protectors of the border areas, the Akrites, as they were known. Their achievements and bravery were lauded in epic folk poetry and songs known as the Akritika (border) epics. In these epics the heroes are attributed with superhuman strength and prowess and the roots of these epics are to be found in Asia Minor, on the Pontos, the Black sea, from where they were introduced to Cyprus. Cypriot bards gave them local colour gaining much popularity for them. Cypriots who suffered much under the raids adopted Dhigenis and the other heroes of the Akritika poems as their own. There are numerous local variations of the names for such heroes such as Dhigenis, Sarajinos, Constantas, Moroyiannos, Haros and many others. Dhigenis has been related to many localities and there are huge rocks still referred to as Petra (stone) of Dhigenis or Petra tou Romiou which is the rock of Aphrodite, and many others.

Arhitecture   The castles, walls and many other forts still pre-
castles and walls   served in all towns, are all examples of Byzantine architecture. Their present form is, naturally, the result of repair and enlargement by the Franks and the Venetians, during the 15th and 16th centuries, but it is very certain that all these fortifications were built on top of Byzantine ones which demonstrate the high degree of Byzantine military building.

We have already mentioned the first of the monasteries established by

The monastery of Saint Neophytos. The Engleistra is situated high up on the cliff. Some of the oldest and most beautiful murals are to be found there.

The Castle at Paphos dates from the Frankish period. The Byzantine one was destroyed in the earthquake of 1222 A.D.

An exceptional location on the coast between Limassol and Paphos, known as "Petra tou Romiou" (the rock of the Greek). Legend says this is the place where the goddess of Love, Aphrodite was born. A newer legend now connects the huge rock in the sea with the stories of the Byzantine Akritic feats.

Monasteries   Sainte Helena and others early in the fourth century A.D., and the organization of monastic life, by Saint Hilarion and others. A tendency of Cypriots towards monastic life was the basic reason for the establishment of a great number of such monasteries on the island. Estimates as to their numbers vary from 52 to 78 such monasteries. This trend gained strength during the raids of the Saracens and Arabs when great numbers of people and clergymen sought refuge in the mountains and lived like hermits. This helped the establishment of monasteries. Governors and army commanders helped maintain such hermit establishments when sent by the emperors to Cyprus during the 11th and 12th centuries, The most historic monasteries, those of Kykko, Macheras, Chrysostomos, Chrysoroyiatissa. They were all built with imperial money under the encouragement of these governors and generals. Despite considerable destruction and damage through the ages, these monasteries still keep their Byzantine character with their guest accomodation around the central churches which bring to mind the early Christian «Agapes» or communities of love.

The first basilicas   There can be no mention of Christian temples as such, before the fourth century A.D., because Christianity was under persecution, and the early Chrisitans did their worship in catacombs. The very first such construction of churches is found in the fifth century. The first such churches built in Cyprus were in the basilica style, which prevailed throughout the Byzantine empire. Church building activity increased during the sixth century and into the seventh, when the Arab and Saracen raids put an end to it. As a result of these raids, many of the churches already in existence were totally destroyed. The ruins of such early Christian basilicas excavated recently (at Lysi, Marathovouno, Athienou, Agia Triada, Paphos, and elsewhere) demonstrate the wealth that went into their construction, in the form of mosaics, wall paintings and frescoes, some of them still in place. The five-isled basilica of Agios Epiphanios at Salamis is very impressive. So was the basilica at Kourion and one recently excavated at Yialousa dedicated to Agia Trias, the Holy Trinity. This one has a unique importance because of its baptistry which is connected to the main building by a series of halls around a courtyard, which were used for many ceremonies and rites preceding the christening or baptism. The whole of th Christening ceremony as practiced in early Christian times, when candidates had to be versed in dogma throughout, upto the entry of the neophite into the basilica itself, became much more understandable with the discovery of this unique baptistry.

Byzantine churches

Cyprus became famous as the Island of Saints and this is related to the strong drive which the Cypriots had to worship God in churches. It is estimated that there were some five thousand churches and chapels from the 11th century onwards. About one tenth of these all boast of some rich or poor example of fresco or mosaic decoration to this very day. The domed, cross-shaped style of Byzantine churches can be seen in a great number of structures throughout the island's villages and towns. A combination of the basilica and the domes of Byzantine churches has survived in two five-domed churches of Agia Paraskevi at Yeroskipou in the Paphos district and that of Saints Barnabas and Hilarion at Peristerona in the Nicosia district. Both are extremely important in the study of Byzantine era church architecture.

Mosaics

The Cypriot mosaic craftsman has given proof that he is the best in the world. The mosaics of Paphos, as well as those in Kourion clearly testify to this. It was, therefore, very natural that this art form was thansrerred to the decor of the chruches. This was practiced in Contantinople and throughout the Bysantine Empire. Mosaics were usually used to cover the apses of the holy altars. When the originals, that is the original churches were destroyed for some reason, the mosaics were thansferred to the new ones. Thanks to this practice we have examples of such mosaics from the sixth century in at least three locations where the churches are, very obviously of a much later date and where the original churches had been sacked during the raids. These are the mosaics of the Virgin of Kanakaria, at Lithrangomi; the Virgin Lady at Livadhi; and the Virgin the Angeloktisti at Kiti. The central motif in all three examples is the Virgin Mary who is situated between the two archangels, holding the Christ. The background is filled by the twelve apostles. The art represented in these three mosaics in of such a high degree that it demonstrates the hight of the crime which led to the destruction of similar mosics at Agios Epiphanios, Agia Triada and at Kourion. Surviving remnants of these mosaics illustrate the richness and excellence of their composition both in mosaics as well as in fresco work.

Frescoes

The most monumental Byzantine art form to be found in Cyprus can be seen in the frescoes. There are some 500 churches from the 11th and 12th centuries, which also incude those built during the Frankish and Venetian occupations, the walls of which are covered by saints, scenes from the Gospels and of the life of Christ, or which bear traces of rich fresco work. The importance of these frescoes, however, does not lie in their numbers, but rather in the tech-

A 7th century mosaic in the vault of the church of the Virgin the Angelbuilt at Kiti. It is one of the best preserved and most beautiful mosaics in Cyprus.

The church of the Virgin the Angeloktisti at Kiti.

Stavrovouni Monastery, which according to the legend was built by Sainte Helene who donated a piece of the Holy Cross to it. It is preserved by the monks as a priceless treasure.

The Church of Saints Hilarion and Barnabas at Peristerona is one of the most characteristic examples of a threeaisled basilica of the 9th to the 10th century A.D. which has three domes over the central aisle, and one each on the side aisles. The five domes form a cross on the roof of the church.

nique used and in their high quality. The Cypriot fresco painter proved to be an excellent discector of the Psychology of the faithful of this time. He inspired them and touched them with his magic in a manner elevating their religious sentiment and made the Christians feel even more Christian. The frescoes in the church of the Virgin Phorviotissa at Asinou, the Virgin of Arakas at Lagoudhera, of Saint Nicholas of the roof at Kakopetria, the Virgin at Trikomo and in the monasteries of Agios Neophitos, Agios Chrysostomos and the Antifonitis, together with those in a series of other chapels and churches are true works of art of incoparable Byzantine style and character with their severe visage of the Pantocrator, the motherly majesty of the Virgin and the calm visage of the saints are very rich in colour which gives them life as if the archangels are about to invite you to join them in eternity.

Icons   The Cypriot painter was just as adept in painting portable icons. The same majestic and calm faces, the harmony of colour and composition as in the many frescoes, give Cypriot icons, mainly those of the 11th and 12th centuries, a purely Byzantine character. When, a few years back there was an exhibition of the «Treasures of Cyprus» which toured several European capitals, and which included examples of Cypriot icon painting, the general impression of the critics was that here we have the art of Constantinople icon painting supplemented with elements expressing the esoteric artistic will of the Cypriot atrist giving this art new life, and making Cypriot icons real pieces of true monumental art.

Other art forms   Cypriot artists and craftsmen also got involved in other art forms, during the Byzantine period. Although we do not have a great number of examles in gold or silver work, ivory of glass making, this is not because these art forms were overlooked, but rather the result of plundering by invaders, pirates and conquerors who prized such items. The few available examples, such as the platters of Lambousa, are superb examples of advanced art and high technique.

Byzantine era the most Hellenic period   As stated earlier, there can be no more erronious argument than that Cyprus lost its Hellenic character because of the raids and its separation from the Byzantine empire at times. These facts in no way altered the ethnologic character of the island. We can find not a single Arabic influenses in the art of Cyprus during those periods. The total and absolute preservation of all elements of the art of Byzantium and the em-

156

pire's civilization in Cyprus only go to prove the degree to which the island as a whole adhered to anything it considered as coming from the ethnic center of the empire, and adopted it. At the same time the empire showed an interest in the island which was not the interest towards a vassal, but interest in a part of the empire itself. This interconnection and relation continued even after the island fell into the hands of the Franks.

The Pantocrator, a mural in the dome of the church of the Virgin of Arakas at Lagoudera which holds exceptional and very fine examples of Byzantine art, considered some of the best in Christendom. 1192 A.D.

The Archangel Gabriel brings the message of annunciation to the Virgin. From the same church of the Virgin of Arakas.

One of the "Tombs of the Kings" at Paphos. All the tombs, as well as their columns are hewn out of the living rock. It is now believed that they are the tombs of many of the officials of the Ptolemaic administration.

The Early Christian Basilica at Kourion. It dates from the 5th cent. A.D.

The Church of the Virgin of Arakas at the village of Lagoudera is considered as one of the best examples of the art of Byzantium throughout Christendom.

The Chrysoroyiatissa Monastery which was built around 1152 A.D. under Emperor Manuel Comnenos, who endowed it with many riches.

The Church of the Virgin Mary Kyra, near Livadi in the Famagusta district. It is built on the ruins of an Early Christian basilica of which only the apse behind the altar is preserved. It has one of the three preserved early mosaics dating to the 6th- 7th century A.D.

An excellent example of silver work which demonstrates the high degree of Byzantine silver work. It is a silver platter of the 7th century A.D. and comes from the treasure of Lambousa. The relief decoration carries a scene from the marriage of David.

The 12th century A.D. Church of the Antifonitis. It´s older frescoes belong to this era while the newer ones come from the 14th century A.D.

The Church of the Virgin Mary Forviotissa at Asinou. It was built by Nikiphoros the Magistros in 1106 A.D. and was decorated with frescoes at his own expense. They are remnants of the best examples of Byzantine art of the 12th century A.D.

The Church of Saint Lazarus in Larnaca.

A detail of the figure of Saint Elias the Prophet, in the dome of the church at Arakas, 1192 A.D.

The Crucifixion. An icon from the Church of Saint Luke in Nicosia. Behind Saint John on the right, we see the centurion who will establish whether The Christ is dead. 13th cent. A.D.

The Dormition of the Virgin. A mural on the Western wall, over the door which leads to the narthex of the Church at Asinou. It was painted in 1105 to 06 A.D. and is thought to be one of the best in colour harmony, execution and the strong Hellenic character of the faces of the Apostles who lament around the Virgin.

The Church of Virgin Mary Chrysopoliltissa in Kato Paphos. Excavations in and around the church have revealed an early Christian Bacilica of Agia Kyriaki. In an adjacent area we have the column of Saint Paul who, fastened on it, received the traditional forty save one lashes. (Saranta para mia)

THE FRANKISH PERIOD 1192-1489 A.D.

ORGANIZATION OF THE STATE

Feudalism   We saw that Richard the Lionheart took half the land holdings of the Cypriots and distributed them as fiefdoms to his officers, thus introducing the feudal system prevailing in Europe during the middle ages. He handed this system over to the Knights Templars when he sold the island to them. The knights, in their turn, handed it over to Guy de Lusignan when they sold the island to him. He organised the system once and for all on the basis of the laws in force in the Kingdom of Jerusalem. According to these laws he divided the fiefdoms into two categories: those with an annual income of 400 Byzants, which he divided among his senior knights who were obliged to follow him in war; and into those with an annual income of 300 Byzants which were divided among the nobles and people of lower rank. Among these there were also those who responded to his invitation and came to settle in Cyprus from Syria, Palestine and Armenia who, by coming, also strengthened the island's defence forces. There were a great number of such people who remained destitute after the Turks conquered Syria, Palestine and Armenia. On coming to Cyprus and receiving the fiefdoms, they joined the ranks of the nobles. Second class fiefdoms were also distributed among the Constables, lightly armed horsemen conscripted locally, who were used to keep law and order.

Fief organization   Fiefs could not be expropriated and were passed on only to legal heirs or through marriage. If the owner died without heirs then the fief went back to the king. Under another law, if Cypriots left the island, and there were many who fled the Frankish oppression, then their land went to the king who organised new fiefdoms. To these must be added the church fiefs which were formed after church property was taken over. This also included monastery lands, subject to the same fate.

Royal authority   The king, like in all the feudal states, was the supreme political and military chief but his authority could be limited by the nobles. He was first among equals (primus inter pares). He was described as the grand noble of the order of the sword. Knights had the duty to defend the rights of the weak, to defend Christendom and fight its enemies and to protect the Sepulcher of the Lord. The maintenance of the court was very costly but it was met from revenues from the Royal fiefdoms which, at the time of the first successor of Guy de Lusignan, amounted to 300 thousand silver Bysants. Minting of coins was the exclusive privilege of the king himself.

The Upper House   The Upper House met with the king and his representative and it was made up of knights and feudal lords who had completed their 25th birthday. It had great powers, including executive, legislative and judicial powers and it approved the ascension of the king to the throne, even though succession was hereditary. It could also appoint a regend if the legal king was under 15 years of age. The upper house dealt with all domestic and foreign affairs and made decisions on peace or war. It had the power to judge all cases brought before it by the nobles, with the exception of those dealing with religious violations which were dealt with by the Low or Nether House. Generally, it limited the king´s authority, laid down state policy and it interpreted the laws, or enacted new ones.

The Low or Nether House   This House was made up of citizens who were appointed by the king. It met under a viscount (knight) and its authority was judicial in cases not involving nobles. The Low House, however, also dealt with disputes or differences between nobles and people of a lower class, or religious infractions.

Officials   The king entrusted the administration of the cities to nobles, but often also to officials chosen from among the citizens. On his coronation the king appointed the seneschal who was a senior official, master of the royal palace and administered and organised court ceremonies. He was also in charge of the maintenance of the forts, and generally he did represent the king in his absence in judiciary and military matters. The king also appointed the Constable, who was second to the king as chief of the army in time of war and handled the affairs of mercenaries. The king also appointed one general to be under the constable´s orders; and a chamberdlain who stood by the king at ceremonies. The position of the viscount was considered very im-

168

portant as he held the post of governor and chief of police in towns and chaired the meetings of the Lower Houses. The positions of admiral, chancellor and Constables were considered inferior.

The classes   Knights and feudal lords comprised the class of the nobles. Immediately below them was the class of citizens, made up of industrial magnates and the merchants. A small number of Cypriots could join this class after the king granted them certain privileges on some occasion. The main citizen body, however, was made up of merchants from Genoa, Pisa, Venice, Marseilles and other parts of Europe who had truly inundated the island. The third class were the subordinates, the Vassals who paid an annual tax of 48 Bysants, as well as one third of their produce. At the same time they were obliged to offer forced labour, that is free work, on the land of their master two times per week. In fact this class were slaves with no privilege at all. Often, some of these vassals earned the favour of their masters who then set them free, and in such cases they did join the classes of the freemen, or francomans. Albanians, white Venetians and white Genoese were special classes with which we will not be dealing here.

Military regiments   The Knights Templars and the Knights of Saint John gained great power and very great influence because of their military orders. The Kings had also granted them many privileges. One of these was the right to maintain their own Castles as their contribution to the island´s security and for their assistance in war operations off the island. The Castle of Kolossi first passed to the Knights Templar and later to the Knights of Saint John in 1307. The two orders also had castles at Chirokitia and at Gastria and their holdings included lands in Paphos, Limassol, and Nicosia as well as in other parts of the island.

Religious Orders   A great number of privileges were also granted by the kings to various religious and monastic orders which had come to settle on the island as soon as the Latin church was established in Cyprus. Among the first of these was the Order of the White-clad Saint Augustine Monks who went to Bella Pais and built there the church and monastery of the Virgin Mary. It still remains one of the most beautiful Gothic monuments in Cyprus. The Dominican Order followed and had seats in Nicosia, Limassol and Famagusta. Most of the Frankish kings were buried in a monastery which this Order built in Nicosia. The Order of Saint Francis, the Fransiscans, as they were known, came to the island nearly at the same time as the Dominicans. They had their seats in the same towns. The Benedictines were also here, and for a time they had held the Monastery of Stavrovouni.

The Assizes Distribution of justice was based on what was known as the Assizes. Originally these were the laws enacted and applied to the Kingdom of Jerusalem. After the Lusignan acquired Cyprus, they amended these laws into a strong legal code for Cyprus. The amendment was carried out on the basis of local customs as well as on the Byzantine laws in force until that time, that is, they were based on Roman Law. Their final form was drafted by a legal expert, John d'Ibeline, under King Hugh the Second.

Guy de Lusignan
1192-1194
Merchant
privileges There are no significant developments under the administration of Guy de Lusignan, which only lasted for 23 months. During this time he was only interested in two things: to overcome the mistrust of the Cypriots towards foreigners, and to repair the castles in the towns and to build other defensive works fearing that the emperor of Byzantium would try to recapture Cyprus. He paid special attention to the expansion and adornment of the town of Limassol in which a large number of European merchants had settled. He granted to these merchants a number of privileges. Guy de Lusignan died childless and before he was crowned king.

Aimery The Upper House proclaimed Guy´s younger brother Aimery as his successor. Upon his coronation he sought to expand and strengthen his power and authority. In the German Emperor Henry the Sixth, he found an ally and a supporter. In his turn Henry sought the support of Cyprus for a new Crusade he was preparing. Aimery´s coronation took place in Nicosia in the presence of a representative of the ally emperor in 1197. The domination of the Franks was established on this date, and it continued to their end.

The Latin
Church A decision by king Aimery to set up the Latin Church in Cyprus proved to be a very serious development as a result of after effects. At Aimery´s request, Pope Celestinus the Third did issue a papal Bull on 20 February 1196 thus establishing a Latin Archbishop of Cyprus with his see in Nicosia. He was to be assisted by three Bishops appointed for Paphos, Limassol, and Famagusta. The Upper House then furnished financial assistance to these three Bishop´s thrones by usurping lands and properties

170

of the Orthodox Church. It also established the Dekati, a special tax on produce, under which one tenth of produce was paid in as a tax. This applied to certain villages and properties which had belonged to the Orthodox Church. Alan, the chancellor of Cyprus was ordained as the first Latin Archbishop.

Aimery also the king of Jerusalem With the approval of Pope Innocent the Third, Aimery married the widowed Queen of Jerusalem one year after his Coronation. With her by his side he was crowned the King of Jerusalem at Ptolemais. But in this he had to shoulder new obligations. He had to liberate Jerusalem from the Turks. His participation in the Third Crusade, in an effort to liberate Jerusalem, and his absence from Cyprus, offered the opportunity to Emperor of Byzantium Alexios the Third, to try and retake the island. He failed, in this attempt, because the Crusaders moved against him and captured Constantnople itself in 1204. Aimery died one year later leaving his under-age son Hugh as successor. Upon his death the Crowns of Cyprus and Jerusalem were separated.

Regency of Guy the First 1205-1218 According to the Assizes the Upper House had to appoint a Regent until the king came of age. As such, it did appoint the husband of Guy's oldest sister, Gautier de mopmeliard. His first act was to put into effect an old agreement between Aimery and Henry of Champagne under which 14-year old Guy was married to Henry's daughter Alice. Knights had the right to marry at that early age. Two years later, Guy was crowned the King of Cyprus in 1210.

Saint Sophia Guy proved to be a very active king. Despite his youth, he took part in the Fifth Crusade, leading his army to Ptolemais and to Tripoli, where in 1218 he suddenly died at the age of 23. It was during his reign that Latin Archbishop Albert laid the foundation stone for the Saint Sophia Cathedral in Nicosia, which was completed in 1228, under Archbishop Eustergius. It remains one of the most representative examples of Gothic architecture in Cyprus. With the capture of the island by the Turks in 1571 it was converted into a mosque and remains as such to this day. The foundation stone for Saint Nicholas cathedral in Famagusta - another excellent example of Gothic architecture, was laid at about the same time. It was also converted into a mosque by the Turks.

The Genoese   When Hugh died, his son Henry was but an infant, and the upper house appointed his mother Alice as regent. In reality, however it was her uncle Phillip Ibeline who ruled the state. One of his first acts was to grant large scale privileges to the Genoese who were masters of a strong and large fleet. His aim was to gain their alliance because he needed them in his efforts to liberate the Holy Land. These privileges included: exemption from taxes on all their goods, whether imported or exported; they were given their own judges, except in cases of murder, theft and treason; certain town quarters in the towns of Limassol and Famagusta were ceded to them. On becoming of age the king ratified these privileges and signed all alliance with the Genoese in 1233. These conditions created by these privileges were so favourable that their town quarters continued to expand year by year, to the extend that in 1373 they laid siege to Famagusta, and with the help of the Republic of Genoa, they enforced their control over the entire island

Attempt to enslave the Church of Cyprus   A historic milestone in Cyprus history was reached in the second year of the Ibelin regency, when he attempted to subjugate the Greek Orthodox Church of Cyprus to the Latin Church. In 1220 Pope Honorius the Third sent Cardinal Pelagius to Cyprus to convene a Synod of the Latin bishops and nobles to decide on how to curb the rights of the Orthodox clergy. A second Synod, two years later, resolved to usurp all Orthodox Church properties, to abolish all Orthodox bishops and to force them to swear allegiance to the Latin church. Reaction was immediate and effective to a point. A delegation was sent to Constantinople to Patriarch Germanos the Second. He intervened strongly and the Latin bishops withdrew their original demands, only asking that Orthodox bishops be cut down to four, a number equal to their own bishops on the island. They also asked that Orthodox sees be transferred to villages as their own sees were in towns.

The Kantara Martyrs   The Martyrdom of 13 monks from Kantara is related to the Latin efforts to subjugate the Orthodox Church, and demonstrates the barbarities which absolute rule and religious fanaticism can bring about, as well as the lengths to which hatred could lead. Two ascetics from Mount Athos came to the island in 1228 in an effort to bolster the faith of the Cypriots. The monks, Ioannis and Konon went to Kantara where they started attracting great numbers of the faithful. This worried the Latins who arrested the two together with another 11 monks and charged them with heresy. After remaining in prison for three years, they were again charged by

Latin Archbishop Eustergius and were found guilty of heresy. They were brought before the Upper House which also found them guilty and sentenced ther to death in 1231. A Latin preacher named Andreas tortured the monks horribly before their execution. The Orthodox Church of Cyprus did canonise all 13 monks as neo-martyrs of Orthodoxy.

Frederick the Second of Germany

Interference by the Latin Church in state affairs became the cause of friction between regent Alice and her advisor Ibelin. This mounted to a total rift and Alice had to leave Cyprus while her friends and supporters worked to overthrow Ibelin. Towards this end they asked for the help of Frederick the Second of Germany. Encouraged by Pope Honorius the Third, Frederick accepted their invitation, particularly since he was planning the Sixth Crusade and needed Cyprus for supplies. In July 1228 we find him in Limassol in command of a strong army and navy.

Frederick Captures Cyprus

Phillip Ibeline, however, died one year before Frederick's arrival and his brother John Ibeline, governor of Beirut, was called upon to deal with the situation. He was appointed Regent by the Upper House and was entrusted with the island's defence. With superior forces, Frederick captured Kition and Nicosia, and forced Ibeline to take refuge in the Castle of Saint Hilarion, from which he surrended. Under the terms of the surrender Ibeline and the nobles had to swear allegiance to Frederick and help him in his crusade. Ibeline was forced to leave the island and go to Beirut leaving the island's administration to five sub-governors appointed by Frederick.

Ibeline returns

Grasping an opportunity when Frederick returned to Germany, John Ibeline tried to recapture the island one year later, when Frederick had signed a truce with the Turks. Although Frederick tried to intervene, Ibeline crushed the enemy's forces near Agridhi on the foothills of Saint Hilarion, demonstrating his strategic genius which gave him prominence among the Latins.

Henry the First

While the war against the Germans was going on, Henry came of age and took over administration officially in 1232, even though he had been crowned king five years earlier. As the king, and with the encouragement of Ibeline he granted even wider privileges to the Genoese who had helped in the battle against the Germans. As a result commerce expanded greatly and state finances revived after the plight of continual wars.

Henry also king
of Jerusalem
Throughout the Latin occupation the Lusignan kings dreamed of only one thing, how to regain the crown of Jerusalem, even though the city was held by the Turks. Amalrich managed to do it for a short time. On the death of his mother Alice, Henry also did it in 1246. Alice had been proclaimed Regent of Jerusalem, and Henry was her heir. However he retained the title of King of Jerusalem only in name for he was never crowned as such. A new barbaric people, the Mongols, attacked and captured the Holy City and the Europeans prepared a new crusade led by King Louis the Saint of France. Henry assisted this new crusade during which the forces of Philip were totally destroyed in Egypt. Henry had played host to the French crusaders in Limassol. He died in 1253 and left his under-age son Hugh as his successor.

Hugh the second,
Orthodox Church
subjugated
Hugh is mentioned as king, but he never reigned nor was he ever crowned. He died at 14 before coming of age. The Upper House appointed his mother Piacensia as regent, but she also died before her son came of age. The Upper House then appointed Prince of Antioch as regent, and his reign, even if only formal coincided with the total subjugation of the Orthodox Church. Latin Archbishop Facianus forced Ortodox Archbishop Alexios and the other bishops to appeal to Pope Alexander, who in a Bull issued in 1260 abolished the Achbishop, and the Bishops were forced to recognise the Pope as leader and the Latin bishops as their superiors.

Hugh the Third
king of Cyprus
and Jerusalem
The first cycle of Lusignan kings ends with the death of Hugh the Second who was childless. Hugh the third, who was the regent, was proclaimed king, and this started the second cycle. Isabella Lusignan, his mother, was also the regent of Jerusalem. Upon her death he was also crowned as King Hugh the Third of Jerusalem. His reign paralleled one of the most critical periods in the history of the entire area. A new ambitious suitor comes up with aspirations of conquest. He was the Soultan Bibar of Egypt, the founder of the Mameluke Dynasty. He had captured Jaffa and Antioch and was threatening Tripoli with a siege. Meanwhile, the various princes who held areas in Syria and in Palestine, as well as the Italian cities with trade monopolies were quarreling between themselves. They were so blinded by their wrangling against each other that they failed to see the danger and unite, in face of the common threat to them all. Hugh went to Ptolemais in a effort to bring about some sort semblance of reconciliation. After he was crowned King of Jerusa-

lem, he also had the right to move forces out of the island. Under the feudal system the lords and nobles who had received fiefdoms from the king, were obliged to fight with him in defending the Kingdom. They did not have to do so in a war of aggression. When Hugh achieved some cohesion among the princes and started military operations in Syria, his knights, encouraged by the Knight Templars, wanted to abandon him under the excuse that the Syrian operation had nothing to do with the defence of Cyprus, where their fiefdoms were. Legal experts who were brought in to advise on the matter, ruled that the knight had to follow the king, and for the first time they were obliged to fight off the island, but only for four months of the year.

Truce with Bibar

Hugh's efforts towards reconciliation of the various princes worried Bibar. On being informed that a new Crusade was being formed by Louis the Saint of France, and Prince Edward of England who, acting on Hugo's advice had signed an alliance with the Mongols. Bibar attacked Cyprus with strong forces. His fleet, however, was nearly sank off Limassol in a storm and some 1,800 of his men were taken prisoners. The blow was so heavy that the Sultan was then obliged to sign a 10-year treaty with the Christians in 1272.

Loss of the crown of Jerusalem

Aspirations on the crown of Jerusalem, an extremely desirable commodity, caused very serious friction among the numerous prices. One of the aspiring suitors was Mary of Antioch who, with the encouragement of the ever-present Knights Templar, worked to gain it even after Hugo was crowned King of Jerusalem, and she plotted to get the decision reserved. Failing in this, she then sold her rights on the crown to Charles of Anju, King of the two Sicilies, who captured Ptolemais, and again with the encouragement of the Templars the nobles recognised him as King of Jerusalem in1277. Thanks to the opposition of the nobles, Hugh failed to regain the crown by capturing Ptolemais. After this the Templars were persecuted by Hugh who deprived them of their castle at Gastria and their properties in Paphos and Limassol. In 1282, however, he was forced to give up this persecution by Pope Nicholas the Third.

Hugh and Bella Pais

Although the Monastery of Bella Pais existed long before Hugh, its existence and prosperity are closely related to him. The church and the monastery were built by the Augustine monks during the reign of Amalrich, when the Latin church was first established on the island. Hugh generously en-

The archaeological site in Paphos known as Saranda Kolones (Forty Columns). A. Megaw, director of Antiquities during the British Administration excavated the city´s Byzantine castle which in all probability was built at the end of the 7th century A.D., to protect against the Arab raids. This castle was completely rebuilt by the Lusignans and was in the end destroyed only a few years later by the strong earthquake of 1222 A.D.

riched the monastery and granted privileges to the monks. One of these was the right to wear a Mitre at ceremonies together with a sword and spurs in the style of the Knights. Hugh the Third was succeeded by his eldest son John, who went to Tyre immediately after being crowned and managed to get himself recognised as the King of Jerusalem, and was crowned as such. The usurper of the throne, Charles of Anju had died in the meantime. John, however, did not live to enjoy his crown because on his way back from Tyre he died after a reign of barely one year.

Mamelukes capture Jerusalem John the First was succeeded to both the Kingdom of Cyprus and of Jerusalem by his younger brother Henry the Second. Holding onto the Kingdom of Jerusalem, however, became a very serious problem. Sultan Bibar´s successor, Sultan Caraum renewed his attacks, and after capturing Laodicea in 1287, he forced Henry to sign a truce similar to the one his father had signed with Bibar. This treaty was violated by the Sultan the very next year when he attacked Ptolemais. The city fell to his successor Sultan Ashraf, after a long siege. Ashraf then proceeded to capture Tyre, Sidon, Beirut, Haifa and Pelerin, the last stronghold of the Christians, and in this way he dissolved the Kingdom of Jerusalem once and for all, in 1291. Many of the Knights were killed during the various sieges, and those who survived came to Cyprus which then filled with refugees, in the same way that the island was filled with refugees during the recent Lebanese war.

Henry´s measures Convinced that Soultan Ashraf would attack Cyprus sooner or later, Henry saw to it that castles were repaired and their garrisons strengthened. He also built additional defence works especially in Famagusta in which most of the Christian refugees had sought refuge. These refugees included Pisans, Genoese, Venetians and Catalans. At the same time, Henry organised raids on Turkish possessions in Karamania, and against the Mamelukes in Egypt and Syria, thus averting an attack on the island. Henry thus concentrated his attention to the island´s reconsturction. This task of reconstruction would have been effective if it were not for the strong jealousies between the various Italian cities, and particularly among these which had aspirations on the Crown of Cyprus. As a result of the fall of the ports in Syria and Ptolemais, the ports of the island gained great importance for commerce. Unfortunately these jealousies between these Italian cities led to clashes between them on Cypriot territory and to family feuds and clashes which greatly delayed or limited reconstructions.

Clash with
Genoese

Rivarly and jealousies were mainly between the Italian cities of Genoa, Venice and Pisa, each one of which wanted control of the Eastern Mediterranean and exclusive control of commerce in the area. In his own desire to give more impetus to commerce, Henry had to extend privileges granted to the Genoese, to the other cities as well, if he was to succeed. Also in an effort to break the monopolies, he granted more such privileges to the Galatans, the Pisans, and later also to the Venetians. Infuriated, the Genoese encouraged pirate raids by their fellow countrymen on Paphos and Limassol, with two of them mentioned in 1312 and 1316. They also allied themselves with the king's enemies and managed to dethrone him for a period. On his return to the throne he took such measures against them that the Pope intervened in order to stop a major clash between Genoa and Cyprus.

Amalric usurps
authority

Domestic clashes, however, also originated within the royal family itself. Henry's younger brother, the vainglorious Amalric, who was the Lord of Tyre and Locum Tenense of Jerusalem, positions given to him by Henry, plotted against his own brother the king, and convinced the Upper House to proclaim him as Governor of Cyprus under the excuse that Henry was an epileptic (1306). He stayed in power for four years and ruled in an extremely totalitarian manner, strengthening his authority by persecuting the king's friends. This made many enemies for him even among his own supporters and aides, and in the end one of them, Simon Montolief murdered him, and Henry returned to the throne.

Abolition of
the Templars

While Amalric was still in power, Pope Clement the Fifth declared the Order of the Knights Templars out of law under the charge that they harboured heretics in their ranks. Execution of the order in Cyprus was entrusted by the pope to Amalrich. In order to gain the Pope's favour and fearing the papal strength, Amalrich brought the Templars to trial, even though they had helped him to overthrow the king, his brother. The trial ended in 1313 when the order was dissolved, and the Knights were thrown into prison in Kyrenia castle. All their property was then turned over to the Order of the Knights of Saint John. Upon his return to the throne, very naturally, Henry had to take strict measures against his plotting opponents. Many were imprisoned in Kyrenia castle, others were exiled and their properties were confiscated. Among these were 460 Genoese who lived in Nicosia. Apart from confiscating their properties Henry kept them in prison until 1320 when on the Pope's mediation he released them. Fearing the Mameluk

A view of the Abbey of Bellapais. It is one of the most beautiful Gothic monuments on the island, admired by thousands. Now it is under the Turkish occupation of Northern Cyprus.

attack, Henry the Second sought powerful friends in Europe. He married Constance of Aragon, daughter of King Frederick the Second of Sicily in 1314, but had no children by her. When he died in 1324 he was succeeded by his nephew Hugh the fourth. Many were enthusiastic about the new king´s character but others, including the Poet Dante considered him bestial. Illness certainly had a great effect on his life and behaviour generally. Jealousies among the foreigners and aspirations within his own royal family, especially when he lost the crown of Jerusalem, became even more complex. Hugh the Fourth followed the policies of Henry the Second for expanding commerce through granting privileges to the Italian cities. This policy had started to give results even before Henry´s death. Hugh extended such privileges to the cities of Florence, Marseilles and to Mompelier, thus turning the towns of Cyprus into cosmopolitan centers of commercial activity. Unavoidably this brought unprecedented wealth, prosperity and luxury to them.

Famagusta   If we are to believe the accounts of travellers, even if only in part, this wealth amassed in the towns, and in Famagusta particularly, must have been legendary. According to one such traveller, " a citizen on betrothing his daughter gave her a present of a necklace, among other gifts, the stones of which were evaluated by French knights present, as more valuable even than the jewels of the Queen of France." Another merchant reportedly sold to the Sultan a valuable scepter with four valuable stones for 60 thousand florins. Later the same merchant offered the Soultan 100 thousand florins to buy it back. The princes, nobles, the barons and the knights in Cyprus must have been the richest people of the world. All this wealth, as described, certainly was not in the hands of the ordinary people who suffered in poverty and misery which was made even worse by calamities such as the floods in Nicosia and Limassol in which five thousand Nicosians and two thousand Limassolians drowned, in 1330. Then came the plaque of 1348 in which chroniclers have estimated that three fourths of the population perished.

Foreign policy   Hugh´s foreign policy was very wise. As the king of Jerusalem, even if only on paper, he assisted all the efforts of the pope and the European monarchs in their various crusades to save the Holy Land. Pope Clemens the Sixth, did describe Hugh as "the bravest defender of Christendom and a champion of the faith."

Yet he took part in war action only once against the Turks during the so called war of Smyrna in which the city was captured in 1343, and stayed in the hands of the Christians until 1402, when it was destroyed by Tamerlane. In 1358 Hugh the Fourth resigned from the throne in favour of his son Peter, who was crowned king the same year. He only lived for one year after his resignation and had spent this year in deep study. Hugh loved philosophy and during his reign he often used to go to country estates, where he withdrew to meet and confer with wise men, like George of Lapithos, and to discourse on matters of philosophy. Renaissance humanist Boccaccio dedicated to Hugh his work "The birthday of the Gods." This indicated the high esteem which Hugh earned in Europe.

Peter the First   One year after Hugh´s death, Peter the First was also crowned King of Jerusalem in Famagusta, and devoted all his efforts to the liberation of the Holy City. His enmity towards the Turks was so great that he used to say that fighting them was a devine mission, pointed out to him in a vision which he received at Stavrovouni Monastery. He founded the Order of the Sword in his efforts to bring his mission to success. The members of this Order wore a special emblem on their chest and were considered among the bravest of warriors. Peter´s military career started in 1361 when the King of Armenia gave him his crown and the fortified port of Kourion. Using the port as a base, Peter attacked Attalia, captured it, and forced a number of Emirs in Karamania to pay him an annual tax. This first success fired his imagination to the degree that he believed that crushing the Turks and the recapture of the Frankish Kingdom of Syria and of Palestine was not impossible. He only needed a new Crusade towards this end, and he started his preparations as his life´s work. Peter devoted the years between 1362 and 1364 to visits to European capitals trying to convince rulers to join the new Crusade. He visited Venice, Genoa, Avignon, where he met the pope, and also went to France, England, Germany, Poland and Hungary seeking Christian support. The result was that a crusade was in fact organised and its forces were taken to Rhodes on Venetian ships. The first forey was organised from Rhodes in 1365. The crusaders were led to believe that their goal were the cities of Syria and Palestine, but Peter had other plans. He believed that if they captured Alexandria, the capital of the Mamelukes, it would then be easy to capture the whole of Egypt and then proceed to the liberation of the Holy Land. His plans were accepted. The attack on Alexandria was such a suprise that the city fell after a short siege, despite its strong fortification. However, on the capture of the city there was such a massacre and pillage, that the whole campaign took on the form of a piratical raid. Peter did entreat the crusaders to continue with their mission but it was in vain. The loot captured in Alexandria was so rich that they considered their campaign ended. After this behaviour Peter was forced to return to Cyprus without fulfilling the purpose of the campaign. He did not abandon his plans. He tried new visits and new efforts to organise a new Crusade but he came up against a strong reaction from the Venetians, who did not want a confrontation with the Sultan, thus endangering their commercial transactions. Peter believed that he would become more convincing if he managed some successes against the Turks on his own. In 1367 he attacked Tripoli, captured, and then destroyed it. He did the same to other cities in Syria and Cilicia from which he returned loaded with loot and full of glory. He failed, however, to overcome Venetian objections and all his efforts for a new Crusade failed.

Peter assassinated   The failure had a great effect upon Peter. He became morose and nervous to the degree of madness. He did not hesitate to violate the laws and to punish the knights without even any respect to their families and their standing. The song of " The Regina and Arodafnousa" one of the most popular of the folk epics of the times, resolves around one of his love affairs and the erotic pecaddilos of his wife Eleanora. His whole behaviour led the nobles to plot against him and, in the end, to have him assassinated, in 1369.

The Vassals   An important development during Peter the First's reign was that a great number of the Vassals were exempted from paying the head tax, and were freed. Peter needed money in order to conduct his war operations. He decreed that the Vassals could be exempted from paying the annual head tax if they paid two thousand silver coins in one single payment. This sum was lowered to one thousand silver coins and then to two hundred silver coins. A large number of the Vassals were able to find such sums and pay up, and so they were freed. Peter the First, most certainly was one of the strongest personalities, not only in Cyprus, but also in Europe of the Middle Ages. He was courageous, enthusiastic and took risks and was very active and mentally agile. Commercial rivalries and the piratical bent of others stopped his drive to contain the Turk and free the Holy Land.

Peter the Second   Peter the First´s son and heir, Peter the Second was only thirteen on his father´s death and the Upper House appointed his uncle John as Regent, despite objections from his mother Eleanora who hated him, considering him an accomplice to her husband´s death. During the Regency, the Upper House, wanting to prevent any future violations of the Assizes, as was the case under Peter the First, appointed a 16-man committee of barons, and eventually all grants of property which Peter the First gave to persons who had no right to them, were annulled, and the house issued a warning that it would not tolerate any further violation of the laws.

GENOESE INFLUENCE 1373-1489

Eleanora and assannins of her husband   The coming of age and the coronation of Peter the Second as King of Cyprus first, and then of Jerusalem, are related to tragic events which led to the final subjugation of Cyprus to the Genoese. These events were the result of the ambitions of Eleanora and her drive to have her husband's assassins punished. In her efforts to get this done, she appealed to the Pope and many kings, but she met with no practical response. She found an opportunity, however, in the coronation of the son Peter the Second in 1371. According to the custom, after the coronation, and during the ride from the church to the royal palace, the Genoese were permitted to hold the right rein of the king's horse while the Venetians held the left. Because the Venetians were more numerous than the Genoese in Famagusta, they managed to have the custom changed and they held the right rein. This gave rise to disturbances during that evening's banquet, and the Genoese were blamed and persecuted on orders from Regent John, while the town's inhabitants looted Genoese shops and homes. This was a golden opportunity for Eleanora who asked for the intervention of the Republic of Genoa, which sent troops to Cyprus under the command of Admiral Pedro Fregozo in 1373. After a tight siege Fregozo caprured Famagusta where he also captured the king and Eleanora, and then he took Limassol and Paphos. After this he started a bestial pillage of all the island's shores. On instructions from Eleanora all of Peter's assassins were captured and killed, with the exception of John who took refuge in Saint Hilarion castle, and undertook to defend it. His brother Jacob took over the defence of Nicosia, but when it was handed over to the Genoese on the orders of the captive king, he withdrew to Kyrenia, which, however, was besieged by the Genoese by land and by sea. This castle of Kyrenia was extremely strong and impregnable, but he was forced to hand it over on the king's request who was forced to do so, with severe beatings. Jacob was imprisoned in Genoa. With the fall of Kyrenia all the castles of Pendadaktylos range capitulated except for Saint Hilarion castle. Being masters of the entire island the Genoese dictated the conditions of the truce to the king. After the treaty was signed and as a result of plots by Eleanora, Saint Hilarion castle was also handed over and John himself was assassinated after she deceived him into coming to the Royal palace.

Genoese treaty Under the conditions which the Genoese dictated to the king, he had to: 1 - pay an annual tax to the Republic of Genoa of 40 thousand gold florins. 2 - to pay to the same republic, in twelve installments, the sum of two million gold florins as war compensation. 3 - The Genoese would live free in Cyprus with the same privileges which Peter the second had granted, and all the merchants would be compensated for damages suffered by them. 4 - As a guarantee for the fulfillment of these conditions, the castle of Buffavento would be given to the Knights of Saint John who undertook to be guarantors for the fulfillment of these conditions. 5 - Also as a guarantee for the fulfillment of these conditions, the port and town of Famagusta and its suburbs was handed over but only for military administration. Results of these adventures were calamitous for the island. In order to meet the obligations which they undertook, the king and his successors were forced to raise taxes excesively. This made them very hated and unpopular to the people, and financially exhausted the country. The occupation of Famagusta by the Genoese, and drive to monopolise trade, forced the other merchants to leave the town and settle elswhere. Many settled in Larnaca which as of that time started to develop and expand to the detriment of Famagusta, which went into a slow decline. This decline could not even be helped by a Genoese edict that all merchant ships must dock at Famagusta, even though in the end this was accepted by Peter's heir James First. All these calamities were the result of the ambitions of a woman who, no matter how much pain she suffered from her husband's assassination should not have enslaved the entire country in order to exact her revenge.

Eleanora's end Eleanora's own ambitions, however, also led to her own destruction. Peter the Second seeking strong allies in his efforts to rid Cyprus of the Genoese, married Valentina Visconte, daughter of the Duke of Milan, who wa allied with the Venetians. Peter was confronted with his mother's objections and this led to an open rift between bride and mother in law, which ended in Eleanora's excile to her native Aragon where she ingloriously ended her life.

A general view of the Castle of Kyrenia from the West.

James the First, new Genoese conditions   We have seen that Peter the Second was succeeded by his uncle Jacob. We know he was held prisoner in Genoa. Before he could rule, however the Genoese forced him not only to sign, anew, the treaty which Peter had signed with them, but they also imposed new, and harsher conditions. These were as follows: Occupation of Kyrenia by the Genoese. 2 - Ceding all customs revenues from Famagusta to them. 3 - All ships were obliged to conduct their trade to and from the port of Famagusta, with the excepiton of ships coming from Turkey, which could use the port of Kyrenia. As an exception the Genoese allowed certain local products, such as charobs to be exported from Larnaca and Limassol. When the new treaty was signed, Jacob was set free to return to Cyprus, and he was crowned king in 1385. Four years later he was also crowned King of Jerusalem and in 1393 he was crowned King of Armenia also. As security that he would be complying with their conditions, the Genoese kept his son Janus in Genoa.

Jacob, the French and the Turks   The reign of Jacob coincides with the last attempt of the Europeans to free the Holy Land. Results of this last of the Crusades were catastrophic for the Christians, who suffered the rout of Nicopolis, on 28 September 1396, in the hands of Sultan Vayazid. Jacob did not take part in this Crusade but he offered to pay the ransom part of it at least, in order to free the prisoners. This earned him the friendship of the king of France. In an effort to gain the friendship of the Turks, to gain time and restore his own finances, he sent valuable presents to Vayazid. This however also forced him to raise taxes. A great number of defence projects are attributed to Jacob, and they give the impression that he was preparing to get rid of the Genoese. He completed the fortificatons of Nicosia, strengthened the castle of Paphos, and that of Kantara, and built a new strong fortress West of Famagusta. He did not have any time to undertake any military action however, because he suddenly died in 1398. The building of Panayia the Eleousa (Virgin the Merciful) is also attributed to him. He built the church as a vow, begging the Virgin to rid the island of the plague of 1392.

Janus 1398-1432   Jacob was succeeded by his son Janus who was crowned king of all the three kingdoms in 1398. His first thought was to retake Famagusta because he saw that loss of this commercial city was a serious blow to the kingdom's finances. In an effort to strengthen his position he married Eloise daughter of Catherine Visconte, Duchess of Milan. Also in order to counter the

Genoese he showed great favour towards the Venetians, who were concentrated in Nicosia, Larnaca and Limassol, which had become the second most commercial center of Cyprus. Janus tried to retake Famagusta twice, in 1401 and 1404. His second attempt lasted for three years and it was during this period that artllery was used for the first time in battle. He failed in both attempts, but he was successful in 1410, when the Genoese tried to take Limassol and were routed. In his efforts to get money, Janus had to impose new taxation but he met great difficulties because of the calamitous scourges which befell the island. Chroniclers describe with horror the plagues of 1409, 1419, 1420 and 1422. In the same vein they describe the three-year attack by locusts which was only ended thanks to measures taken by Janus for destroying the locust eggs.

Janus and piracy European merchants had elevated piracy into a systematic business because of the high profits. Seeing this, Janus encouraged the Cypriots to follow the example of the Europeans in pillaging the Sultan's holdings. They started to practice this to such a degree that they became a scourge for the Sultan, and the shores of Cyprus became havens for pirates, from which they carried out their foreys. Reaction from the Sultan of Egypt came in 1424 when he settled certain domestic situations which had not allowed him to act earlier. With a small force he captured Limassol, and then turned towards Paphos which he took very easily. On his way to Paphos he also sacked and destroyed the sugar cane plantations at Kouklia. He returned to Alexandria loaded with booty, but he came back the next year with a stronger force. With the help of the Genoese in Famagusta they captured Kalopsidha, and then Larnaca, destroying Kellia on their way. Aradippou, then Dromolaxia and Kition followed. He returned to Alexandria with even richer booty and thousands of prisoners. The Sultan's 1426 operation was the most destructive. Foreseeing the attack, Janus sought the help of the Europeans, but the Sultan, fearing a new Crusade against him, acted first. With a strong army and fleet he besieged Limassol, capturing it in two days. Janus moved against him and in a clash near Khirokitia his army was in such a confusion, that the batle became a massacre. Janus himself was wounded and taken prisoner. The Sultan then marched on Nicosia, which was handed over to him by the nobles in an effort to aviod bloodshed. He took Larnaca with the same ease, and the entire island capitulated to the Sultan. His troops then started looting, pillage, arson and the massacre of the people. Destruction was unprecedented. On leaving Larnaca the Sultan took with him mythical wealth in booty and six thousand prisoners with wounded Janus among them.

Peace treaty   The Europeans, naturally, were concerned over the turn of events. If the Mamelukes became masters of Cyprus, this meant that all commercial avenues would be closed and even the survival of the Byzantine empire would become problematic. For this reason they intervened, or rather forced Janus to come to terms with the Sultan and to sign a peace which also included the payment of war reparations in the amount of 200 thousand dukats and an annual tax of five thousand dukats. This was to be paid in silken cloth, known as «Idaré», the manufacture of which must have been flourishing, if we are to judge by the terms of this treaty. The Europeans extended a loan to the king so that he could pay his war reparations.

Efforts to return the bishops   This was the tragic state of affairs to which the king led the island by his encouragement of piracy. Janus died of depression in 1432. During his reign there were two attempts by the Patriarch of Constantinople to have the Cypriot bishops returned to the bosom of the Eastern Orthodox Church. We have already seen that in 1260 Pope Alexander the Fourth had issued a Papal Bull forcing the Cypriot bishops to recognise the Pope as head of the Church. The Partiarch had twice sent his personal envoy to Joseph Bryennius in 1405 and 1411 to convince the Cypriot bishops to disavow the Pope, but his efforts failed. This may illustrate the conditions of dire suppression under which the Orthodox had to live during the Frankish domination.

John the Second 1432-1458   Janus was succeeded by his eighteen-year old son John the Second king of all three Kingdoms in 1432. Because he was rather effeminate and soft character, while times were very difficult, the Upper House also appointed Peter Lusignan as Regent. Peter, who was also the Count of Tripoli was also given a council of four nobles to supervise and direct primarily foreign affairs until the king became 25 years old. The regent's first act was to reaffirm the island's obligations in an effort to guarantee a period of firm peace during which to restore the country's finance which were in dire streights. However, jealousies between the Genoese and the Venetians, which continued, was an obsacle to this revivalist effort. The strong occupation of Famagusta by the Genoese did not help matters. Apart from depriving the state of strong and lucrative revenues, it also had repercussions on the relations with merchants from other Republics who had to be taxed, despite the privileges of tax-free operation granted to them by other kings. In this way, these financial problems did not permit adoption of measures to cope with a new threat by the Turks against the island's independence. This gap was filled by the Europeans in answer to an appeal by Pope Nicholas the Fifth. Some sent money and others troops to defend the island, while the Pope financed the navy which, under the command of King Alfonse of Arragon, was stationed at Rhodes with orders to protect the two islands, the only ones remaining in Christians hands. The danger of invasion of the island was thus averted and Cyprus remained outside the world - shaking events which led to the dissolution of the Byzantine Empire, and changed the course of history.

John the Second and Helen Palaeologou   The family life of John the Second played a very important role to the history of Cyprus. His very wedding was a matter of exploitaiton by people who, counting on his weak and soft character wanted to marry him to a woman, who with her influence, would have served their own interests. This explains the multitude of marriage offers received by the king in 1437. In the end he married Medea, the daughter of John-Jacob Palaeologus, Marquis of Momferrat. She, however, died two months after their marriage. He then married Helen, or Elena Palaeologou, daughter of Theodoros Palaelogos the Second, Despot of the Morea and Duke of Sparta, who was the second son of Emperor Emmanuel Palaeologos of Byzantium. Elena Palaelogou is related to very serious developments in the history of Cyprus. Elena Palaelogou, a genuine Byzantine princess was, without any doubt, one of the bravest personalities in Cypriot history. Witty and sharp of mind, very active and with great aspirations she was both wise but also sly and extremely faithful to Orthodoxy. She played a leading role in a great number of developments which her soft husband could never have handled. The failure to elevate her foster brother Thomas to the rank of Cardinal, led her to clash with the Pope because Thomas was Orthodox. This did not deter her, but on the contrary strengthened her deternination to restore the Orthodox clergy whom she supporte continually, both financially and morally. She was extremely nationalistic and, after the fall of Constantinople to the Turks, she took under her own protection many Greek refugees whom she settled in the Monastery of Mangana which she had richly endowed. She never gave up a cause until she won. Her greatest achievement was her appointment as Regent by the Upper House. She virtually ruled the country from this post.

Jacob, illegitimate son of John   Elena failed only once in forcing her will upon the king. Apart from Charlotte the legal daughter he had with Elena, John also had an illegitimate son, Jacob,

The Castle of Kantara on Pendadaktylos Range.

Saint Hilarion Castle. Even today, it´s role was considerable for the success of the Turkish invasion.

whom he adored because he was learned and active. Fearing that her daughter Charlotte would be swept aside, Elena asked that he be removed. In this, however, she achieved the exact opposite because John installed him in the Palace of the Archbishop, and contrary to objections by the pope himself he ceded to his son all the income of the Archbishopric. Jacob played and important role from his position, and even managed to become king. The marriage of Charlotte to John Coembr, grandson of the king of Portugal in 1456, led to a series of incidents with dire consequences for Helena. She had insisted on the marriage but in her son in law she met a fanatical Catholic who all the time desagreed with her actions towards restoring the Orthodox clergy. The rift between them was so great that the couple were forced to leave the Royal Palace. One year later John was found murdered and Helena's foster brother Thomas was thought to be responsible. This incident gave rise to a very serious inter-family tragedy from which the king's illegitimate son emerged as the winner. Charlotte allied herself with her illegitimate brother who assassinated Thomas and the nobles who supported him. When the Upper House wanted to punish him, his influence and charm used on the king was so great that not only was he not punished, but the Archbishopric was once again given to him. From this position he became extremely powerful and used his influence against Helena. An example of her downfall was her failure to prevent a second marriage by Charlotte to Louis of Savoy, a marriage opposed also by the Orthodox Church. This affected her health and she died in 1458 the same year during which John the Second also died, leaving the throne to Charlotte.

Charlotte
1458-1464 rift
with Jacob

Before his death, John named his Daughter Charlotte as his heiress and she was crowned in 1458. However, his bastard son Jacob, was considered dangerous to the crown. The nobles did not want him on the throne, and they convinced Charlotte to have him removed, from the position at the Archbishopric where his father had placed him. This was the first grave mistake committed by Charlotte, and in the end it cost her the throne. Jacob would not give in easily. After a plot he had concocted with some of his friends to overthrow Charlotte, failed, he escaped from Cyprus with his friends and took refuge in the Sultan's court in Alexandria. He convinced the Sultan not only to recognise him as the legal king, but also to help him retake, as he alleged, the throne. In September 1460 a strong Egyptian fleet arrived before Ayia Napa, where a part of the army landed. The rest went to Larnaca where Jacob and the main force landed and he immediately received support from many of his followers and a great number of villagers. His advance was very rapid and he captured Nicosia without a battle. Charlotte and Louis who had taken refuge there, abandoned the town and went to Kyrenia awaiting help from the West. Using part of his army and fleet Jacob besieged the town, and with the rest of his forces he besieged Famagusta. The sieges of the two towns went on for four years. During this time, by contrast to her soft husband, the Queen Charlotte moved in every direction seeking help. She was on the move all the time, sometimes in Rhodes seeking help from the knights, then in Rome seeking support from the Pope, other times in Venice begging the republic not to help Jacob and at other times in Genoa and Savoy. The help from Savoy was considerable, especially after an agreement that if Charlotte and Louis died without heirs the crown would go to the Duke of Savoy. The Dukes of Savoy later called upon this treaty many times.

Fall of Kyrenia Despite tha many promises, however, assis-
and Famagusta tance was not large enough to stop Jacob. The sieges became so tight that it became a matter of how much time the people could last without food. The garrison of Famagusta came to terms in 1464 and the city was handed over thus putting an end, once and for all to the sovereignty of the Genoese upon it. The capitulation of Kyrenia followed. The commander took advantage of Charlottes absence in Rhodes and reached an agreement with Jacob and so Jacob became master of all Cyprus in 1464. Charlotte, however, did not accept the situation without reaction. While in exile from Cyprus she increased her efforts to retake the island. She had great charm and met with understanding and promises everywhere. Pope Sixtus the Fourth even did her the honour of having her painted in the Chapel of the Holy Spirit, kneeling before him and receiving his blessing. Things, however remained at the level of promises. Developments coincided witn the increased power of Venice whose interests in Cyprus could be served much better by Jacob. Nobody dared run the risk of a war with Venice in order to return Charlotte to the throne of Cyprus. All the efforts of the dethroned queen came to an end in 1474 when even the king of Naples Ferdinand, abandoned her. It was then that she took the historic decision and transferred the crown to the Duke Charles of Savoy in 1485. After two years of quiet life, she died in Rome in 1487. It is not known whether Jacob was ever crowned king of Cyprus. He bore the title however from 1460 when the Sultan recognised him, and as king he proved himself a very wise monarch with political acumen. He forgave his enemies and to many he presented a great number of his own holdings, thus cutting the royal revenues. He thus earned the esteem of the nobles. Under his policies the country's finances began to improve, as did learning after he invited many teachers and artists from abroad to the island, and founded schools.

VENETIAN IFLUENCE

Catherine Cornaro, daughter of the Venetian Republic   Venice had every possible interest in displacing the Genoese and placing trade into her own hands. The Doges were very astute and clearly saw the imminent collapse of the Francs on the island. They cultivated close ties with the King. During the siege of Kyrenia, Jacob became close friends with two Venetian nolbes, Andrea and Marco Cornaro. The Venetian republic exploited this friendship and saw to it that Jacob married Catherine, daughter of Marco Cornaro, and proclaimed her as «Daughter of the Republic of Venice» in an official ceromony in Saint Marc's Cathedral. The importance of this act was very great. It meant that if Jacob died without an heir, the crown would go to Catherine and then to the Rebublic of Venice which, as a foster mother, got inheritance rights over Cyprus, after Catherine's death. This diplomatic act gave Cyprus to the Venetians for 80 years. The wedding was performed in 1472 and one year later Jacob died on his return from a hunting trip, and left Catrhrine pregnant. According to his will the heir to the throne would be the child to be born by Catherine. This fell right in with the plans of Venice. As a foster mother the Repubic got an active interest in the protection of the queen and her unborn child. On instructions from the Republic, the Venetian admiral read a proclamation to the people, under which the queen and the security of the island were placed under the exclusive protection and care of the Republic of Venice, thus making the island a Venetian possession.

Charlotte reacts   Charlotte, however, who was still living, tried to make things difficult for he Venetians. She had numerous friends and supporters both inside and out of Cyprus, with king Ferdinand of Naples at their head. With their help she tried to retake the island. With the Catalans on her side, because their interests would have been affected if the Venetians prevailed, Charlote managed to become the mistress of the situation, but only for a moment. The Venetians with their strong fleet and great influence on large masses of people on the island, soon put a final end to Charlotte's ambitions. When the heir was born and baptised in August 1473, the Repulic of Venice saw to it that he was crowned as Jacob the Third, when he was barely three months old. It still remains a mystery whether the death of Jacob the Third at the age of one year, was a natural one. What is well known is that upon his death Venice appointed two councillors and one overseer to advise the queen, and these gentlemen took over all authority from her. The documents of the Republic, which survive, addressed to the councillors, are nothing but orders from the central government to the administrators of a colony. These dealt with orders to strengthen garrisons, replace commanders, repair of castles, handling of finances, and generally on the administration of the country. The control of Venice was so absolute that it even set the queen's annual income at eight thousand ducats. This period of Catherine's reign must however, be considered only a transitory period leading into Venetian domination.

Foreign affairs   The foreign affairs of Cyprus were always regulated in accordance to the interests of Venice. The position of the Republic between the Sultan of Egypt and the Sultan of Turkey was very delicate. The two had very hostile relations towards each other. Venice accepted the vassal tax to Egypt, and undertook to pay it. At the same time, however, it did not want to reach a rift with Turkey, whose intentions to capture Rhodes and Cyprus were very clear. When in 1468 the Sultan of Turkey, Vayazid, asked the Rebublic for permission to muster his fleet in Cyprus while campaigning against the Sultan of Egypt, Venice found herself in such a difficult position that not even her notorius diplomacy could save the Republic from Vayazid's wrath. Taking the Republic's hesitation as an alliance with Egypt, he attacked Famagusta. Even though the attack failed, it made Turkey's final intentions all too evident. The ceding of the crown by Charlotte to Charles of Savoy, greatly worried the Republic of Venice. It's concern became even graeater with the discovery of plots against the life of Catherine and after information that Ferdinand of Naples was trying to marry the queen, or some other lady descended from the Lusignans in order to gain rights upon the throne. Thus the republic wanted to speed up its conquest of the island and convinced Catherine to resign in the Repubic's favour. Her brother George Cornaro and Admiral Francisco Priuli, who were sent to the island towards this end, had no difficulty in convincing her after the attempts upon her life. On 26 February 1489 the queen handed over the banner of Saint Marc to the Venetian commander, and it was raised over Famagusta, as well a in all other towns of the island. The official Venetian occupation of the island started on that date. Catherine's official resignation took place on 20 June in Saint Marc's Cathedral. The republic endowed her with a rich pension on which she lived in historic luxury until her death in 1510.

ARTS AND LEARNING UNDER THE FRANKS

Chroniclers   The writing of chronicles was cultivated by the Cypriots during the Frankish years. This was natural because the Cypriots, both the clergy and others, living under constant pressures and restrictons, could not have created any serious spiritual work. This applies more to the bishops who, being subjugated to the pope, could not write freely, being under the threat of being charged as heretics. It is also questionable, even though the chronicles offer no indication, whether two of the writers of chronicles whose work survives, Leondios Macheras and George Vostronio were also connected to the royal court. Leondios Macheras had very close ties with Janus, and members of his family, like Peter Macheras, and they were used on diplomatic missions. Leondios himself fought side by side with the king in the battle of Khirokitia. His chronicle which is a most important historic document on the island under the Franks goes upto the death of Janus in 1432. Vostronio was a close friend and aide to Jacob the Second who encouraged learning on the island. His chronicle ends in 1501. Their chronicles gain a special interest as they both had lived at close quarters with political affairs of their times. Apart from objectivity, which can be checked from other sources, their chronicles show an attempt not to stray away from the feelings of the people, the customs and mores and traditions of the people which are described in a lucid and living language. This is why their chronicles also have a literati valve as they both use the peoples dialect, thus giving us the opportunity to study it, together with the influence this language had on the Frankish language. The same literaty importance can be attributed to the Assizes which were also translated into the peoples dialect of the Cypriots. Their study gains special importance because they also incorporated in the principles and customs of Byzantine times.

**Other men
of letters**   George Kyprios was another Cypriot who excelled in religious writing, but he blossomed only when he became the Ecumenical Patriarch. Bearing in mind the recent martyrdom of the 13 monks of Kantara, he fought with all his strength against the movement for the unification of the Orthodox and the Latin chuches during the reign of Emperor Theodoros the Second known as Laskaritis. The fact that the movement was a failure thanks to the efforts of a Cypriot Ecumenical Patriarch was the strong reason for the well known Bull of Pope Alexander the Fourth which subjugated the Church of the island to the Latin Church. Mention must also be made of George Lapithis the philosopher who had close relations with Hugh the Fourth. Unfortunately we have no examples of his work.

196

The Crucifixion. A mural on the Western fronton of the Church of Agios Mamas at Louvara. The church was decorated with frescoes in 1465 A.D.

The virgin between Archangels Gabriel and Michael. A mural in the Church of the Virgin of Podithou at Galata. Painted in 1502 A.D.

The Crusifixion. A mural in the church of the Virgin Podithou at Galata from 1502 A.D.

The Ascension. A mural from the Eastern dome of the Church at Arakas. 1192 A.D.

198

Folk poetry   With the arrival of the Franks on the island, the Cypriots were introduced to new customs and mores, new social systems in the life of the kings and the nobles and the princes in court and in all its luxury and wealth. All these things, by contrast to their own very conservative life, were sung by folk bards, and they have survived from mouth to mouth even to our own days. Among the most sung is the song of «The Queen and Arodafnousa» which deals with the loves and amores of Peter the First and with the jealousy of Eleanor. The «Cloth Vendor», the «Zografou» and the «One Hundred words» belong to the same cycle of folk poetry, and song.

Architecture   The churches are the only architectural monuments from the Frankish period. The Franks, in their efforts to impress the Cypriots, and attract them to their own religious dogma, built very impressive churches. Those of Agia Sofia in Nicosia, Saint Nicholas in Famagusta, the Monastery of Bella Pais, are among the most beautiful of Gothic monuments. Despite all their efforts, however, they did not manage to impose their style, except in a very small number of cases. Of these we have the Church of Saint George of the Hellenes in Famagusta. The Cypriots continued to build their own churches in their own national Byzantine style to the degree that some of the most beautiful Byzantine churches belong to the time of the Frankish domination.

Frescoes and icons   Where we can see a clear Frankish influence in Cyprus is in the frescoes and icons of the churches. The painting of the period of the renaissance has such vitality and beauty, that the Cypriot painter could not avoid it in his painting and icons. He very adeptly combined the Byzantine painting mentality which had become a passion for him, with the classical painting of the renaissance which he learned from the Franks. He painted masterpieces of religious art which decorate the Byzantine churches of the fourteenth and fifteenth centuries, which are admired by the experts.

Working in gold   If one is to judge by accounts of travellers about the wealth of merchants, one can conclude that working in gold and precious metals must have been very advanced. All accounts praise the wealth of jewellery which filled the shops in Famagusta. It is however doubtful, but perhaps, more likely that the makers were Cypriots.

An icon of Saint Andrew of the 15th century A.D. now in the monastery of Agios Neophytos.

The national feeling   We will analyse the policy followed by the Franks and the results of its application. This is a very lengthy period of pressure and trials, a period during which the Cypriots suffered under the humiliation of their oppressors who, after enslaving the people, tried to deprive them of every trace of personal freedom and revenue for life. Hunger, misery, lack of happiness were the main characteristics of the life of many Cypriots throughout this lengthy period of three centuries. All these things, however, were not enough to bend the national feeling which was revitalised and bloomed by the appearance on the throne of two genuine Greek ladies, Helena Paleologou and her daughter Charlotte, which changed the rhythm of the realm and gave it a purely Greek and Christian hue. When the Franks left Cyprus, one could not have believed that after three whole hundreds of years, they would leave no trace of their passage apart from a number of Gothic churches and a few Frankish words on the genuine Greek language of the land. Leontios Macheras and George Vostronio, the two Cypriot chroniclers who were honoured by the rulers, thought and felt like Greeks in a way that they become a luminious example of national resilience in this land, and of the peoples virtue which never lost its national aura, even after honours and positions were bestowed upon them.

Victory for the Chruch   The triumph of the Church was equally as great. The pressures of the Latin Chruch for the purpose of subjugating the Cypriot Church and in order to proselyte the people, cannot be measured. The martyrdom of the 13 Kantara monks speaks for itself. Usurpation of Church Properties, suppression of the Bishops, Bulls and excommunications by the Pope, none of these could bend the religious beliefs of the people and their fervour, which demonstrated their determination to remain faithfull to the religion of their forefathers. It is certain that the Bishops accepted the Bulls of the Pope Alexander the Fourth, but it is even more certain that their recognition of the Pope in no way drew them away from Orthodoxy which they maintained as a dogma despite all the pressures towards the contrary. Only a small spark was needed in order to restore this giving in of the Bishops. This spark was provided by an infidel, the Sultan Selim the Second, who, by conquering the island in 1571, freed the Church of Cyprus and liberated it from the oppression of the Latin Church and of the Pope, by restoring its autocephalus character.

VENETIAN OCCUPATION 1489-1571

New administration
The transfer of the island to the Venetians also brought with it a change in administration. The throne and the Upper House were abolished. These were virtually abolished ever since the death of Jason the Second when the Venetians took over authority. Executive authority was held by the Locum Tenense and the two advisors on a two-year term of office. Their powers were great and extended to administration generally, to the judiciary, defence and financial administration. In excercising their duties, they had at their disposal executive officials who were directly appointed from the Republic of Venice. Finances were handled by two cashiers or Key-bearers. In the judiciary there was the Viscount assisted by 12 deputy judges elected by the citizens both Greeks and Latins. Justice was meted on the basis of the Assizes, but the entire process was now conducted in the Italian language which had replaced the French. The translation was entrusted in 1513 to a committee of legal and language experts among whom we find Florio Vustronio, brother of George Vustronio who continued to write his chronicles in Italian. The legislation was kept upto date continually, but this was the sole responsibility of the Republic of Venice which alone had the right to legislate.

Imrpovement of Nicosia defences, and those of Famagusta
Because of the many enemies surrounging Cyprus, the Venetians showed a very special interest in organizing the military affairs of the island and in strengthening defence. Because the manning of all defences was both difficult as well as costly, they overlooked some of them and devoted their efforts to strengthening the ones most important for defence. Among those which were overlooked were the castles of the Pendadaktylos range, which were abandoned in 1562. Also for the reasons of cost the castles of Paphos and Limassol and to a degree the castle of Kyrenia, were also overlooked. Their entire interest was concentrated in the castles of Nicosia and Famagusta. They started to work towards strengthening their defence right from the start. Famagusta had a special importance for the Venetians and they appointed a general to oversee its defence. The local Locum Tenense and the

Kolossi Castle in Limassol district. It has had many masters, Byzantines, Knights Templars, knights of St. John who were also it´s last masters to use it as a castle.

advisors could not in any way interfere in his work. In times of peace it was his duty to oversee the repair and strengthen the walls and the city's garrison. In some instances he took on the title of General of Cyprus, which meant that his duties also covered the defence works of the other towns and destricts. Two garrison commanders assisted the general of Famagusta. In times of trouble or war then the Republic appointed an overseer whose military authorities were very extensive.

Grand Council of Nicosia   With the abolition of the Upper House, it was very natural that the nobles were disgrantled and they also reacted against the administration. In their effort to countr this, the Venetians appointed the Grand Council of Nicosia on which sat all the nobles who has completed their 25th year of age. All Venetian citizens living on the island also had the right to sit on this Council. Its task was to cooperate with the goverment on certain matters of administrative and judicial nature, and to appoint junior officials.

Export trade   The Venetians did much in order to expand the island's export trade. Competition, however, created many problems and difficulties. We can see this mostly in the case of sugar, produced in sugar cane plantations at Kolossi, Episkopi, Achelia, Kouklia, Emba, Lapithos and Morphou. Trade in sugar was one of the profitable forms of commerce. At this stage, however, it could not compete with Portugal whose production in Madeira was much greater. For this very reason they were forced to uproot the sugar cane plantations and instead to start planting cotton, for the first time on the island. Cotton at that time was also a basic export commodity. Cotton, together with wines and salt from the salt lake at Larnaca, a very much sought after item, were the basic exports of the island.

A blow to the silk manufacture   A decision by Sultan Selim the First to collect the vassal tax in cash , was a severe blow to the economy. The Franks had agreed to pay this tax to the Sutlan of Egypt in the form of silk cloth, idare as it was known. This tax, however was turned over to the Sultan of Turkey for cash payment. While the tax was paid in idare, this gave a great boost to the island's silk industry, and this in turn gave a boost to silk worm cultivation. Both these branches of the silk industry went into decline when the tax had to be paid in cash on the demands of Sultan Selim. If to all this we add the serious calamities which befell the island during the Venetian era, we can then understand the great difficulties the Republic had in finding revenues, from which to pay both for defence, fill its coffers, and also help the republic itself. Thus the republic was forced to seek new sources of revenue. The Venetians questioned the validity of certain grants by the kings to nobles, they reorganised the feudal holdings many of which turned up in the hands of the government. The government earned considerable sums of money be selling them to Cypriots. Another way of finding new funds, was to grant freedom to settlers who were now willing to pay for it. In this instance, however, we have an indication of the poverty on the island. Although the sum needed was rather low, very few of these settlers were able to pay it.

Harsh administration All these difficulties, coupled to the need to hold on the island due to important interests, turned the administration of the Republic of Venice into a harsh tyranny. Travellers who did visit the island under the Venetians, all speak of the dire poverty of the people and the harsh measures of the Venetians in their efforts to find money. Property, honour, reputation, the personal freedoms, all these were so easily trampled by the Venetians that a general ferment grew up on the island, often expressed in riots, and in one case, even in an appeal to the Sultan for protection. The Venetians resorted to all these measures in order to terrorize the people and in order to achieve, as they believed, the perpetuation of their occupation of the island and at the same time to supply their republic with funds.

Foreign policy One of the first actions of the Venetians, was to get recognition of the island's transfer to them, by the Sultan of Egypt who was considered the sovereign power, since the kings paid a vassal tax to him. This tax was also recognized by the Rebublic of Venice which undertook to continue to pay it. This convinced the Sultan to grant his recognition of the transfer. Settlement of affairs with the Sultan in Constantinople, however, was much more difficult. This was because of the enmity between the two Sultans. Because the Turks had to deal with the Persian danger, they were forced by events to sign a peace treaty with Venice. This act of the Venetians proved to be beneficial. When in 1509 Pope Julius the Second organized the Coalition of Cambrais, incorporating a number of European rulers into a movement against Venice, the united fleets of the Pope, of Spain and of France, did not dare attack Cyprus because of this very alliance of Venice with Egypt and Turkey.

**Turkish danger
Suleyman the
Magnificent**

Things started to change, however, in 1516, the year when Sultan Selim the First conquered Egypt. The Venetians were obliged to recognize the Sultan of Turkey as sovereign, and to pay him the vassal tax, and even in cash, as we have already seen. When, a short time later, Selim's heir, Suleyman the Magnificent captured the island of Rhodes in 1522, when the island was under the Knights of Saint John, who were dispersed, then the danger for Cyprus increased, and became obvious. The question became not if the Turks would conquer Cyprus, but when they would do so. In order to gain time, as the Turks had captured from them their Aegean islands and their last holdings in the Peloponnese in Greece, the Venetians were forced to sign a degrading treaty with Suleyman, recognizing his sovereignty over the captured areas. What Suleyman the Magnifficent did not achieve, was done by his successor, Selim the Second in 1566. He first of all entrusted Lala-Mustafa Pasha and Piali Pasha with the organization of a strong army and navy, having appointed them general and Admiral. He then sent an ultimatum to Venice demanding the hand over of Cyprus in order to avoid the shedding of blood. It was natural that the Republic firmly rejected the ultimatum, and together with preparations for defense it asked for help from the pope and of the Europeans in order to save the last Chrisitan outpost in the Eastern Mediterranean. Pope Pius the Fifth, who clearly saw the chasm to which the Western world was led by the jealousies of its rulers, made a last ditch effort to unite Europe in a common war against the Turks. For a moment his efforts appeared to be succeeding as Phillip the Second of Spain undertook to help Venice with 150 ships. These ships, together with 12 from the Pope and 148 Venetian shipswere an extremely strong armada which would have made the capture of the island impossible for the Turks. Unfortunately, the commander of the Spanish fleet Jovanni Doria, after many delays which are considered deliberate, made sure that the fleet was only ready to sail after the fall of Nicosia on 9 September 1570.

**Larnaca falls
Nicosia
besieged**

On 1 July 1570, Piali Pasha with 350 ships and more than 100 thousand men was off Limassol. Landing a small force he captured and looted it and did the same to the Monastery of the Cats, the one known as Saint Nicholas of the Cats. The Venetian commander of Paphos, however, moved against him and forced him to move to Larnaca where he landed all his forces under General Lala-Mustafa Pasha. The Turks were met with no resistence because the local commander Nicola Dandolo had decided to face the Turks in Nisocia. A few days later Lala-Moustafa was before the city and besieged it with 100 thousand men. He boasted he had 200 thousand in the siege. The siege of Nicosia continued from 25 July to 9 September 1570 and the defenders did not number more than 10 thousand men under Nicola Dandolo who proved to be unable to take any intitiative. Lack of discpline, inadequate distribution of food and ammunition, squabbles between officials, the absence of any courage for foreys out of the walls, were the characteristics of the town's defence. In the end Nicosia could not hold out. When the walls were breached, the first Turkish standard bearer set up the Turkish flag on Constanza bastion, and was killed immediately. To honour him Lala-Moustafa Pasha erected a mosque on the site, now known as the mosque of Bairakdtar, the standard bearer's mosque. The fall of Nicosia was followed by a massacre and looting. Dandolo and the Bishop of Paphos were among the first to die. Victims of the massacre have been estimated at some 20 thousand men women and children. On 12 September Saint Sofia church was turned into a mosque, and it has remained as such to this day. The prettiest young women with a great amount of loot were sent to Famagusta and were loaded into ships to be sent to the Sultan as a gift. Among them was Maria Singlitiki, who performed an act of heroism described as the greatest in Cypriot history, when she set fire to the ship's powder armoury in an effort to escape slavery. Thus she and the flower of Cypriot womanhood were blown up to bits together with the Turkish ship.

The siege and fall of Famagusta

On the fall of Nicosia all the other towns surrendered without a battle with the exception of Famagusta. Lala-Mustafa then besieged it, using all his forces, by land, while Piali Pasha besieged it from the sea. The siege went on for more than ten months, from 16 September 1570 to 1 August 1571. The city's defence was directed by General of Famagusta Marcantonio Bragadino, Supervisor Ectore Balliane and the General of Paphos Laurentius. Contrary to what happend in Nicosia, with only seven thousand defenders, with wisdom, courage and strategy, they managed to repell repeated and fierce attacks by the besiegers whose numbers were being continually increased, reaching a total fo 250 thousand. The defenders also ogranized daring foreys during which some 80 thousand Turks were killed. Generally they brought the enemy to a very difficult position. When everything had been exhausted, strength, food and ammunition, when the walls were breached in many places, only then did the defenders raise a white banner asking for conditions of surrender. It was agreed. One, that Venetian officers and men with their arms, five cannons and their families and luggage should board ships which would take them to Crete. Two- Any of the Greek and other fighters wanted to do the same, could do so. The remainder would go free and be masters of their properties and their religion would be respected. As soon as the city was handed over, the Turks reneged. They executed Ballione, put Marcantonio Bragadino to tortune and went on a looting spree which lasted for days. Lala-Mustafa Pasha took the booty to the Sultan himself. He, however, arrived in Constantinople on a day of great mourning. It was on 7 October 1571 the day on which the Turkish fleet was routed at Naupaktos. This result, in no way affected the fate of Cyprus which remained a Turkish possession. This was also officially recognised by the Republic of Venice by a treaty on 7 March 1573. The fall was also mourned by a peoples bard in «Cyprus Lament» which has survived from mouth to mouth to our own days.

TURKISH OCCUPATION

ADMINISTRATION AND THE CHURCH

New administrative structure After the Turkish conquest, Cyprus and four other Sanjaks, or possessions, in Asia Minor became the seat of a Beyler-Bey who was the supreme official or the governor of the island. Immediately under him there were four Aghas, who, together with the Beyler-bey and some of the other officials made up the Divan, a form of a State Council according to the model of one that was operating in the capital, Constantinople. The Agha, who was below the Beyler-bey , was responsible for financial matters. Then came the Agha of the Janitssaries, who took the place of the Beyler-bey first Beyler-bey. Muzafter Pasha was appointed and the island was subdivided into four administrative districts, each one of which had subdivision, five in Nicosia District, and four each in the districts of Paphos, Larnaca and Kyrenia. The Limassol district belonged to Nicosia. These districts which became six at the end of the Turkish occupation have been the basis for today's six districts.

The Cadi Responsibility for matters of religion and justice were concentrated in one official, the Mullah as he was first called, or the Cadi as he came to be known later. The Cadi of Nicosia was the senior one, and according to the chronicle of Archimandrite Kyprianos, he was the keeper of, and defender of the faith as well as judge in cases of a personal nature, loans, title deeds for property and so on. He had authority to impose sentences upto flogging, the well known punishment of fourty and one lashes. His salary amounted to 15 thousand piasters paid by the inhabitants of the five subdistricts of Nicosia. The Cadis of the other districts had similar authorities but their salaries were lower and they were obliged to pay either to the Cadi of Nicosia or to the sublime porte a percentage of what they were entitled to collect from the people as their salary. The operation of justice was based on the Koran which was law to them, The one, who interpreted under what law of the Koran the trial would take place, was the Mufti who issued the so-called fetvah or interpretation of the law.

External and domestic security

The defence of the island against external dangers was entrusted to a force of one thousand Jannitsaries and 2,666 horsemen known as Spahis. The second in seniority Agha, was in command of the Jannitsaries. It is not certain whether child collection had applied in Cyprus, because the Turks had abolished the practice even before they captured the island. A small naval force was also stationed in Famagusta and controlled the situation. Maintenance of domestic law and order was in the hands of the Zaptiehs who were commanded by Soubashi, or the Cavalry commander. When the British took over authority in 1878 there were a total of 275 Zaptiehs on the island.

Taxation and the Kharadch

In order to pay the salaries of all these officials the Turks imposed a number of taxes, which the people could not bear. There was the salt tax, the water tax, the tax for Cadis salaries, the tax for officials and the military services, and the most hated tax of all, the head tax or the Kharadch. The Kharadch was paid by all males from 14 to 60 years of age and it was based on the property condition of the citizenry who had been divided into three groups for this purpose. In 1572, and for reasons of taxation a census of the population was held and it was found that there were 85 thousand males between the ages of 14 and 60. On the basis of this number the island's population in the first year of the Turkish occupation has been estimated at 197 thousand. These various forms of taxation and the heaviness of the taxes, coupled to the pressure which tax collectors did subject the people to gather the taxes, forced many Cypriots to abandon the island to the degree that the population continually decreased. The results of this population decrease were two-fold. Either the decrease in taxes collected, which led to a budget deficit which in 1585 was estimated at 68 thousand dukats which the Porte was forced to pay, or the resultant increase in taxes on those who remained behind. This made the Turkish rule tyranical and hated. It becomes obvious that the Soultans would want to prevent emigration by citizens in their effort to forestal an economic collapse. They had to adopt such protective measures in order to provide for economic improvement. In this effort they tried to encourage the inhabitants to purchase feudal holdings which had once belonged to the nobles. In this way they also hoped to increase both cultivation and production. The Churches and the Monasteries were also encouraged to buy back the lands usurped from them by the Latins. These measures, did not produce results, either because local officials did not implement them, or because continuation of the heavy taxation neutralised the good intentions of the Sultans.

Restoration of the Autocephalus church of Cyprus   One thing that one could particularly point out is that the Turks, even though they were non-Christians, they did not interfere in the conduct of religion by the Orthodox inhabitants. This was not the case with the Latins, whose churches were converted into mosques. The Orthodox kept their churches with only the use of bells prohibited. The Orthodox also welcomed into their churches any of the Latins who wanted to follow mass. It is also characteristic that right from the first year of the Turkish occupation, the Turks allowed a meeting in Constantinople of the local Synod made up of the Ecumenical Patriarch, the Patriarchs of Alexandria and of Jerusalem, 53 Metropolitan bishops, which, once again gave its recognition to the Autocephalus Church of Cyprus. It also restored the Archepiscopal throne of Cyprus which had been abolished by the Latins with the Bull of Pope Alexander the Fourth. The Senior Canon of the Great Church Timotheos was elected the first Archbishop. He was a Cypriot and came from Kykko. At the same time, the metropolitan bishops were allowed to return to their original sees in the towns instead of in villages. An explanation of this Turkish behaviour must be found in the strong influence upon the Porte in Constantinople by the Ecumenical Patriarch and the Fanariotes.

Filotheos mediation 1754   With the passage of time the Archbishop and the Bishops won certain privileges and won power and prestige not only among the Christians, but also among the Turks. In 1660 the Porte recognised them as Agha-Vekili, or mediators, and protectors of the Greeks, or Ethnarchs as we would call them today. In this capacity they had a right to submit the complaints directly to the Porte through the dispatch of missions. One such mission was the one of Archbishop Filotheos who, with the Metropolitan Bishops of Paphos Ioakim, Makarios of Kition, and Nikiphoros of Kyrenia, managed to win very important privileges. In his document, known as the Hat-ti Humayun, the Grand Vizier set the amount of the Kharadch and other taxation at 20 and a half piasters and the monastery tax at four thousand piasters, to be collected by the Bishops who would hand them over to the governor. They were also recognised as Kodjabashi, that is protectors of the rayas. This mission greatly enhanced their powers.

The Institution of Dragoman   The Institution of Interpreter or the Dragoman, was adopted right from the first years of the Turkish occupation. The Dragoman was nominated by the Archbishop, and after the approval of the Governor, he was recognised by the Sultan in a special firman. The Dragomans were commis-

An icon in Phaneromeni Church in Nicosia, with the portrait of Dragoman Hadjiosef, his wife Anna and their two children. They are protected by the Virgin and the Archangels on either side of Her.

Portrait of Hadjigeorgakis Kornessios wearing his official uniform. In his left hand he is holding a firman with the Sultan´s signature, thus confirming his unlimited power.

sioners of the people, they conducted the population census, valued the properties, and in collaboration with the Archbishop they imposed taxation based on the property value of each one. They had to approve the budget of the island and they had the right to report directly to the Porte, any deviation by the authorities. In order to be distinguished from the other officials they had a special uniform. It becomes obvious that with all these responsibilities and duties they also acquired great power. Whenever there was a concord of views between the Dragoman and the Archbishop they often managed to overthrow decisions by strongman governors, and restore a more just administration.

Hadjigeorgakis Kornessios Numerous Dragomans worked to protect the Greek inhabitants against the rapacious appetites of governors and Aghas. Christofakis and Hadjiosef are mentioned among these but particular reference is made to Hadjigeorgakis Kornessios from Kritou Terra. His term of office coincided with a period of domestic upheaval as a result of the greed of Chadji Bakki Agha who ruled in such a tyranical manner from 1777 that a revolt appeared imminent. The situation was saved by Hadjigeorgakis who managed to go secretly to Constantinople in 1784 and with the help of some of his very powerful friends there, including the Oecumenical Patriarch and Alexander Ypsilantes, grandfather of the commander of the Holy Brigade during the Greek revolution, Alexander Ypsilantes, he managed to have the island freed from a hated governor.

1804 revolution In 1795, Chadjigeorkadjis was made a lifetime Dragoman by the Sultan. He gained such power that he could even dismiss Governors and Aghas by a simple personal recommendation to the Porte. His influence became even greater when he married Maroudia, the sister of the Archbishop of the time Chrysanthos, who also had a great influence, particularly after the signing of the treaty of Kuchuk-Kainardji in 1774 under which Turkey recognised the Tsar of Russia as protector of the Orthodox Christians in the Ottoman Empire. This excessive power, however, fanned the hatred of the Aghas against both of them, a hatred which was fanned by the French consul because both Chadjigeordjis and Chrysanthos followed a pro-Russian policy relying on the Tsar´s protection under the treaty. This hatred broke out into a revolution in 1804, when the infuriated crowd broke into the Archbishopric, manhandled the Archbishop who was barely saved by steward Kyprianos, his future successor and Ethnomartyr. The crowd went to the house of Hadjigeorgakis who, however, had escaped with his family. They ransacked it in disappointment. When the Dragoman reached Constantinople he convinced the Porte to send two Pashas against the insurrectionists, with two thousand Jannitsaries from Karamania. Payment for the mercenaries would be supplied by the Archbishop. They did suppress the revolution, and against the efforts of the French consul they severely punished the revolutionaries. This punishment was the cause for Hadjigeorgakis' own end. The French consul was in continual correspodence with the French ambassador in Constantinople who managed to influence Turkish policy from 1806. He demanded the removal of the Dragoman and curbs on the Archbishop's powers describing them both as the greatest enemies of France. At the same time the relatives of the executed insurgements also clamoured for revenge. It was easy for them to slander the Dragoman of plotting and to have him condemned to death by the Vezeer, who was a great enemy of Hadjigeorgakis at the time of great tribulatons for Turkey - The Turco-Russian war was still on and the Treaty of the Dardanelles had just been signed by Turkey. Britain had also just also declared war on Turkey. The Russian and British ambassadors tried and managed to get a firman from the Sultan sparing the life of the Dragoman. They rushed to the vizier, but it was too late. Hadjigeorkakis was already dead. Thus a very great and brave personality in Cypriot History ended his life in the midst of the jealousies of the aspiring successors of the Ottoman Empire, France, England and Russia.

Donations by Hadjigeorgakis and his wife

Many donations by the Kornessios couple are on record. Among other there a number of donations to churches, building of churhces in Aglanjia and Agios Dhometios, renovations of churches, grant of lands in Nicosia, where the British later built the Leper Hospital and the current Pedagogic Academy, piping water to Nicosia, the donation of a farm in Kythrea to the church of Agios Antonios, financial assistance to the Monastery of Chrysorogiatissa, a donation of ten thousand piasters to the Greek school in Nicosia established at Hadjigeorgakis own expense by the monk Ioannikios on the site of the Present Girl's High School of Phaneromeni.

Administrative changes

On the recognition of Greek independence and at the end of hostilities, the great powers demanded administrative changes · from Turkey, leading to more liberal conditions in Cyprus. In 1830 there was a new recognition of the Archbishop and the Ethnarch bishops of the Greek people in Cyprus. At the same time a constitution was granted, providing for the election of certain elders in the capital, and other towns to Councils with various powers. In 1838, Mahmoud the Second who became known as the Peter the Great of the Ottoman Empire amended the constitution for more liberalism with greater participation of the locals in administration, since now they could also be members of the Divan. The most important reforms, however, came in 1856 when the Turks were obliged to recognise and grant basic freedoms to all their subjects. These freedoms were granted by a High Decree known as Hatti Humayoun, which gave all the Sultan's subjects irrespective of race or religion, equal political and civic rights. Under the High Decree, two Councils were formed. They were the Idare Medjlis and the Judiciary. The Idare Medjlis in the capital Nicosia, was made up of 13 members with the moutesharif, as the governor was known as the president, the Mufti, the Mullah, three Turkish officials, the Archbishop and six citizens elected by the people, that is three Greeks and three Turks. The composition of the provincial Idare Madjlis was similar. The elected members here were four, two Greeks and two Turks. The Judicial Council was made of the Cadi and four members, two Greeks and two Turks.

Civic rights   The High Decree granted citizens civic rights, such as election of their representatives to municipal councils in the towns. They were responsible to oversee matters of health, town cleaniness, town planning, water supply and other matters. They also had the right to elect the councils of elders, the chairman of which was known as the chief elder and on the Turkish ones he was known as the Mukhtar, a term which has prevailed on both. Two years later in 1858, the High Decree was supplemented with new reforms, one of which was acceptance of the oath of the Christians in the courts. Under the same reforms, the Bishops had the right to register the movable and immovable property of Christians who had died, leaving underage children. The Archbishop particularly received the right to build a bell tower at Saint John's Cathedral and to use bells for religious ceremonies. The reforms of 1858 were the last granted under the Turkish administration.

UPRISINGS BY GREEKS AND TURKS

1578 uprising   It became obvious right from the first years of Turkish administration, that the situation for the people would not be better than before but on the contrary, thanks to the rapaciousness of the authorities, which, as we have seen, neutralised all good intentions from the Sultan, would become even worse. Every time this rapaciousness rose to the levels of pure robbery, the people rose seeking more humane treatment. Such an uprising occured only on the seventh year of Turkish administration. It was of such an extent that the Beyler Bey was killed by his own Janitsaries because he held on to their pay.

Demands by the
Duke of Savoy

At the same time, the West never lost it's appetite for retaking Cyprus. The Venetian were not the only ones interested. The main contender was the Duke Charles Emmanuel of Savoy to whose house Charlotte had transferred the crown. He sent to the Porte his demand that Cyprus should be given back to him as the legal heir to the crown. When, as expected, the Porte rejected his request, he came into contact with the bishops asking for their help to retake the island with the promise of a constitution in 1600. The plan was never put into effect because the Turks came to know about it and strengthened all garrisons. By contrast to the Duke of Savoy, Duke Ferdinand of Tuscany in 1605 did attempt to retake the island sending a strong fleet for this purpose. He found the Turks well prepared, and his weak forces, which landed near Famagusta, were massacred. Bearing in mind the experience of Ferninand, Charles of Savoy later rejected demands from the Cypriots themselves, first from Peter Goulemis, the first Dragoman, in 1608, and later, in 1609 and 1611, from the Archbishop and the Metropolitan Bishops who promised him every help if he undertook a campaign to liberate the island. The same fate befell an appeal by Archbishop Nikiforos to the Duke of Savoy in 1670, which was also the last such appeal. On this failure, the Cypriots gave up any hope that the West would liberate the island and stopped making appeals to the West.

Revolt against
Chil Pasha
in 1765

Although the Cypriots gave up hope for help from the West, they none-the-less never stopped fighting on their own for an improvement of their conditions of life and for a share in the administration. The revolt against Chil Osman Pasha is one of the best known. In 1754 Chil Osman, the governor , raised taxes by 44.5 percent for the Greeks while for the Turks the percentage was only half that amount. He also used violent means in collecting the tax. Archbishop Paisios and the Bishops protested and they managed to have a representative of the Grand Vizier to be sent to Cyprus. He found their complaints justified and invited the representative to come to him so that he would announce his decision. Chil Osman, however pretended to be ill and asked the representative to come to the Saray to make his announcement. At the same time he also invited the Aghas, the Mullah, the Archbishop and the bishops together with a large number of elders, Turks and Greeks alike, all numbering about 300 persons. His real purpose was to assasinate all of them and remain master of the situation. This can be discerned from the fact that when the Grand Vizier's representative was on the point of making his announcement, the floor of the Serai collapsed and the Archbishop and a number of those invited fell through into the basement and were injured. When an investigation was held, it was found that the supports of the floor had been sawn through by hand on instructions from Chil Osman. Thus the weight of the guests caused the floor to collapse. All those present, Turks and Greeks alike chased Chil Osman, cut him to pieces and also looted his property and destroyed whatever they found in the Saray.

The Halil revolt 1766 In its effort not to permit any repetition of such events, the Porte even though it recognised that Chil Osman was responsible, did enforce a special tax on the people in order to compensate the family of the governor and for the damage caused to the Saray. The Greeks paid the tax under heavy pressure but the same did not happen with the Turks. They took up arms against the tax collectors. This turned into a revolt under the garrison commander of Kyrenia, Halil Aga, who placed the entire island under his own control. The situation for the Christians now became worse because they found themselves between two fires. They sent a mission to Constantinople under Archbishop Paisios who succeeded in having two Pashas sent against Halil, and they suppressed the revolt in 1766.

Hadji Bakki Agha The administration of Hadji Bakki Agha was even harsher. His very name inspired terror to many generations even after his death. He had only one eye, was repulsive to look at, and came from Klavdia in the Larnaca area. He was a wood cutter by profession. This wood cutter with his plots managed to rise to the highest position in 1777 and to keep it until 1784. Throughout this period he did greatly oppress the people. The Bishops protested in vain against the unbearable taxation and the inhuman methods used by his men in collecting the taxes. The situation fostered another revolt but Hadjigeorgakis Kornessios intervened by visiting Constantinople with the Archbishop and the bishops and achieved his dismissal. In the end he died of the plague.

THE GREEK REVOLUTION AND CYPRUS

Archbishop
Kyprianos
Archbishop Chrysanthos was succeded to the throne by Kyprianos, whom we met as the Archbishop's steward who saved the Archbishop's life during the uprising of the Aghas in 1804. He was born in Strovolos and received his first education at the Monastery of Macheras. In 1783 he went to Wallachia to collect funds for the monastery and there he met Voivod Michael Soutsos, who recognised his many attributes and kept him there for further study. He returned to Cyprus in 1802 and he was offered the administration of the Macheras Monastery annex in his native village of Strovolos. Later he was appointed as steward of the Archbishopric. A man of education himself, he fought illiteracy and on ascending to the throne he established a Greek school opposite the Archbishopric. Classical studies were the main subject at the school. The school was completed in 1812 and was dedicated to the Holy Trinity. In 1893 the Pancyprian Gymnasium was built on its site.

Filiki Etaeria
In 1818, Stergios Hadjicostas or as he was known Hadjistergios and Demitrios Ypatros, both officials of the Philiki Heteria (the Society of Friends) arrived in Cyprus in order to initiate the Archbishop into the Society, together with the Bishops and a number of elders. The Archbishop presented strong reasons why Cyprus should not join the revolution, with the small distance separating the island from Turkey as the main one. The grand assembly of society members in Ismailia in 1820, found these reasons valid and agreed that the contribution of Cyprus should be financial.

Nikolaos and
Theophilos
Theseus
Going against this decision of the Society, two enthusiastic members - who had settled in France - Nikolaos and the Archimandrite Theophilos Theseus decided to come to Cyprus and incite the Cypriots against the Turks. In April 1821, Theseus came to Cyprus bringing with him letters and proclamations, some of which fell into the hands of the Turks. They tried to arrest him but he escaped to Greece where he excelled himself, together with his brother, rising to the rank of the Lieutenant General. His brother was in command of the foreign volunteers who came to Greece to help the cause but who had no leader.

Above: A bust of Ethno-Martyr Kyprianos in the courtyard of the Archbishop´s Palace.

Below: A bust of Archbishop Sofronios in the courtryard of Saint John´s Cathedral in Nicosia.

Kuchuk Mehmet reaction   The discovery of the proclamation naturally created concern for the administration of Kuchuk Mehmet, who, found an excuse to neutralise the power of the Archbishop and the bishops whom he feared. He immediately asked the Sultan for reinforcements and approval for the execution of 486 elders, whose wealth and relations with foreigners off the island, made them dangerous. The Archbishop and the metropolitan Bishops topped the list. The Sultan was favourable to two appeals by Kuchuk Mehmet, because he did want to restore the morale of the Turks with one succesful blow in Cyprus. At that time the Turks were suffering severe adverse defeats in the Peloponnese. So Sultan Mahmoud approved boht the list and sent four thousand men to Cyprus.

The tragedy of July 9   With the Sultan's firman in hand, Kuchuk Mehmet used sly means to gather most of those on the list at the Serai and the July the 9th tragedy of Cyprus commenced. Archbishop Kyprianos was hung from a mulberry tree on Serai Square. Archdeacon Meletios was hung from a plane tree opposite him. The beheading of the metropolitan Bishops started on the same day and went on until 14 July. Metropolitan Chrysanthos of Paphos was first, followed by Meletios of Kition and Laurentios of Kyrenia. Then followed the Bishops of Kykko and Agios Chrysostomos Monasteries and other elders. A total of 470 people were executed, fewer than on the list because some managed to escape with the help of consuls of foreign powers.

TRANSFER OF CYPRUS TO THE BRITISH

Aspirations of foreign powers   The position of Cyprus has been such that the island became very necessary for those who wanted to control the Middle East. The same applies to this day. There were numerous countries which, right through the eighteenth century, when it became obvious that the Ottoman Empire was on the wane, had many aspirations on the island. Among them were Russia, France and England, mostly England which wanted to safeguard the way to its most important possession, India. The campaign of Napoleon the Great in Egypt had this very purpose in 1798: to cut and prevent the passage of the English towards India. The fact that France failed, did not mean that the danger was averted. The same danger did appear in 1856 when the Russians in the Crimean war of 1853-56 crushed the Turkish fleet near Sinope and forced their two fanatical adversaries, the French and the English to join forces against Russia and to force it, after the stronghold of Sebastopol fell, to sign the Treaty of Paris in 1856 prohibiting Russia to have any fleet in the Black Sea.

Russian expansionism policies The Russian position in Cyprus was very strong thanks to the Bishops, and the favour they showed towards Russia. The reason for this favour was the Kuchuk Kainarci treaty which ended the Crimean war, and under which the Sultans recognised the right of Russia to be the protector of the Orthodox in the Ottoman Empire. This right was often exploited by Russia because it inspired the enslaved people under the Turks to believe that with Russian help they would be liberated. The other European powers, with England and France in the van, naturally reacted to this Russian expansionist policy, and this led to the Anglo-French coalition against Russia and to the Treaty of Paris.

Cyprus-England prior to 1878 The aspirations of the British on the island were once again encouraged by the Bishops and Hadjigeorgakis Kornessios, because England, although not as friendly as the Russians, was not hostile like France. Enmity towards the French was the result of their support to the Franks and the Catholics. After what they had suffered under the Franks, the Bishops could not come to terms with the French. This is why the English were certain that occupation of the island by them would not be opposed by the people. Before 1878, the Britain had an opportunity to occupy Cyprus in 1832, when the Sultan offered the island as guarantee for a loan in order to suppress the revolution of Mohammed Ali, the Pasha of Egypt. Because England was among the guarantor powers which had recently settled Greek-Turkish relations, it was forced to reject the offer, even though it was a unique opportunity for a base protecting the way to India. There are reports that the same offer, with the same results, was made to England in 1845.

Secret Anglo-Turkish Accord An offer in 1878, however, had a different fate. The Turkish-Russian war of 1876-1878 ended in a Turkish defeat and Sultan Abdul Hamit was forced to sign the Treaty of Saint Stephen which gave Russia so many privileges that it became the strongest power in Europe, causing serious concern to all the other European powers which reacted immediately. They asked for a revision of the treaty, and this was done by the Treaty of Berlin in July 1878. The English, with a more successful diplomatic activity received the occupation of Cyprus. Under a promise that England would support Turkish interests at Berlin, and an obligation undertaken for English help to Turkey if it was again attacked by Russia, it signed a secret accord giving them Cyprus, to be used as a British base against Russian expansionist plans. This secret agreement was supplemented by a second agreement on 1 July, which regulated the details of the first accord. The sixth and last clause of this supplementary agreement provided for the return of Cyprus to Turkey as soon as Russia returned Kars to Turkey together with some other portions of Armenia. The importance in the addition of this clause is self evident. In its effort to forestall natural reaction from the other powers, England wanted to present the ceding of Cyprus as a temporary measure for protection of Turkish interests and not as a permanent occupation of the island. There is no doubt however, that when Salisbury signed the agreement, his sole purpose was to keep the island for ever as a base in order to protect British interests in India and the Middle East. The third clause of this supplementary treaty provided that England should pay to the Porte the surplus of the budget, based on the average of the last five years. After hard bargaining, this was set at 93 thousand pounds.

Recognition of the transfer On 12 July 1878 a squadron of the British navy under Admiral John Hay, arrived off Larnaca. It was only then that the other powers were informed about the secret agreement, while they were meeting in Berlin. It was by then too late for any reaction since the ceding of the island was undertaken voluntarily by Turkey in order to seal the agreement. On the day after Hay's arrival in Larnaca, the final treaty between Russia and Turkey was signed in Berlin, and the other powers were in no position but to accept transfer of the administration to England as a fait accomplis on 13 July 1878. This transfer ended the Turkish presence on the island which had lasted for 300 hundred years. The fact that Hellenism survived through this period is due to the bravery of the dragomans and their power and the power of the Bishops which forced respect of Orthodox rights. The Orthodox church never came to know as much power as it had earned under the Turkish occupation. To this power is attributed the fact that Cypriot Hellenism maintained its national spirit and its religious sentiments intact, survived and defeated the conquerors.

THE BRITISH OCCUPATION 1878-1960

Administration   Sir Garnet Wolseley arrived on the island on 22 July 1878, and on the next day he was sworn in as the High Commissioner and Commander in Chief of Cyprus. This title was born by the representatives of the British throne until 10 March 1925, when the island was declared a British colony. After this day they bore the title of Governor, and they Kept it until the end of the English occupation on 16 August 1960. Wolseley was welcomed by the local inhabitants at Larnaca, because they saw the British as liberators. The speech of welcome by the Bishop of Kition Kyriakos is characteristic. He stressed that the Cypriots accepted the change in administration believing that the British would repeat their gesture for the Ionian islands and that they would help the island unite with mother Greece. There is an attribution of this wish to Archibishop Sophronios in his address to the High Commissioner on his arrival in Nicosia on 30 July, but the most probable thing is that Sofronios only referred to the expectations of Cyprus for justice and equality and for an active participation in the administration, through a constitution.

Legislative   Foundations for the first Cypriot constitution were
Council   laid by a Royal Decree of 14 September 1878. It provided for the establishment of two councils of the island. A legislative council and an executive council. The Legislative Council was made up be the High Commissioner as its chairman and by not less four or more than eight other persons of whom half would be officials, Englishmen, and the other half locals, Greeks and Turks, or by Christians and Moslems, as they were defined. The locals were to be appointed by the crown on the recommendation of the High Commissioner, who was also authorised to legislate laws and issue decrees on the basis of a joint decision of the Legislative Council and the approval of the crown. The crown had every right to reject any law or decree and replace it with another with the approval of the Royal Council. In case of an emergency the High Commissioner was given the right to legislate emergency laws and decrees on his own, but their duration was stipuraled for six months only. The High Commissioner also had the right to dismiss any

members and replace it with another in a way which made the authorities of the Legislative Council very shadowy.

Legislative Council 1882   The authority of the Legislative Council remained shadowy as it was reformed on recommendations from the Greek population. The number of members was increased to 18, with six official members and the other 12 elected. Nine were elected by the Christians and three by the Moslems. Cyprus had been divided into three election districts and the Turkish subjects had the right to vote. (All Cypriots continued to be known as Turkish subjects upto 1914 when the island became a possession of the British Empire). The right to vote came into effect at the age of 21 when the subjects paid a certain amount of tax. However, both in the Legislative Council of 1878 and the one of 1882, the Grand Governor had the tie vote in case of an equality of vote. This happened very often, because the Council's composition with the combined votes of the official members and the Moslems balanced those of the Christians. The Moslems were also displeased because they considered their votes too low by comparison to those of the Christians. They reacted with memorandums to the English and Turkish governments. The Christians, mostly Greek, also were displeased as they considered the Council's composition a mockery, since their equality against the combined official and Moslem votes, gave the Grand Governor the right to cast the winning vote in such a way that on matters of policy the Christians were unable to impose their will. Reaction from the Greeks was very strong and it was not limited to the House. It even reached the British government with memorandums and missions.

Legislative Council 1925   With the declaration of the island as a Crown Colony on 10 March 1925, the composition of the Legislative Council was also amended. Members were increased to 24 with the addition of three official members and three Greek members. Things did not change, however, since the winning vote remained with the Governor as he came to be know from now on, and the equality of votes between the official and Turkish votes on the one hand and the Christian votes on the other. Reaction from the Greek members became stronger from this time on. Memorandums and missions followed one another untill the Christian members resigned with the 1931 movements as a sequel.

Abolition of the Legislative Council   Abolition of the Legislative Council was the direct result of the movement of 1931. The island came to be ruled under the governor's decrees and

224

laws. From 1934 onwards he formed an Advisory Council of four Greeks and one Turk who would advise him in enacting laws. There was a general outcry against both Greeks and Turks who agreed to become members of this Council at the time when the island's politicians were working towards the re-establishment of the Legislative Council on a better basis.

Lord Winster's mission Despite all efforts and even pressure in the British Parliament, it was not until 1946 that the British government mennt decided to discuss the matter of a consitution for Cyprus. Towards this end Lord Winster was sent to the island in October 1946. His mission, however, was extremely difficult because by then, the demand of the Greek inhabitants for Enosis, (Union), with Greece, was at its climax. Cyprus had offered a lot of blood from its sons during World War Two, side by side with the British as did Greece, which was considered a pioneer in the victories against the Axis, and later in the resistence. This is why both Cyprus and Greece expected a fulfillment of their aspirations. Denial of this fulfullment led the Archbishop Leontios to denounce the Winster mission and he called on all Cypriots not to attend the consultative conference which was called in order to discuss the new constitution. After this denunciation, which was repeated by Leondios' heir, Makarios the Second, the conference failed and Cyprus remained without a constitution or any representation until its independence.

Winster's provisions for a Constitution Failure of the consultative conference was not the result of reaction from the Greeks alone, since some of them did attend. The failure was the result of the character of the constitution itself. Despite improvements, it had continued to give the Governor such authorities, that it lost all meaning of self rule. The proposed constitution provided for a House of 26 members of whom four would be officials (the Colonial Secretary, the Attorney General, the Chief Accountant, and the Commissioner of Nicosia) of an equality of votes was circumvented. However, it also incorporated unacceptable restrictions. For example: 1- The position of Cyprus within the British Commonwealth could not be debated within the House. 2- Legislative Bills related to finances, defence, foreign affairs, with the minorities and the constitution, could not be introduced for debate without the approval of the Governor. 3- The Governor had the right to reject a law if, according to his judgement, it affected public order or the administration of the country. Naturally, it is right and proper to have such laws but the most appropriate agency to decide, is not the Governor but the Legislative Body.

Executive Council   The Declaration of 13 September 1878 also provided for an Executive Council the members of which, and their number, were regulated by the British government upto 1925. Usually there were five members with the Grand Governor as Chairman, but he was not obliged to ask for the council's advice. In 1925 the number of members was set at seven, of which four were officials (the Governor, the High Commissioner, the Attorney General, and the Accountant General) and three unofficial members, two Greeks and one Turk, to be appointed by the Governor either from among prominent citizens or from members of the House. But, even under the new composition, the Governor did not have to consult the council for advice at all times.

High Commissioner administrators   Second to the Grand Governor in the government apparatus, was the High Commissioner who, after 1925, came to be known as the Colonian Secretary. He stood for the Grand Governor in his absence, and chaired the meetings of the Executive and Legislative Councils, whenever the Grand Governor was in no position to attend the meetings. Administration of the districts was in the hands of Commissioners with the Commissioner of Nicosia as their senior. When in time services demanded an administrative re-adjustment, it was necessary to appoint District Inspectors, and later, Assistant Commissioners. These last posts could be held by local residents, Greeks and Turks, but the posts of Commissioner were reserved for the British. Heads of Departments were also reserved for the British. Their fuction approximated the function of Minister. Such posts were the Director of Education, Agriculture, the Director of Antiquities, Public Works, Mines, Forests, Labour, Land Registry and so forth. From 1878 to 1931 both Greeks and Turks fought hard for appointment to these higher posts but they succeeded only in very rare instances.

Municipal Councils   It was noted that after the Treaty of Kuchuk Kanardji, the Turks had granted to the Greek inhabitants rights of participating in local Councils, Municipal and Elders Councils. These rights were even strengthened by the British improved legislation. Municipal Councils were set up in all towns and in the larger villages. These were elected every four years, and were responsible for all sectors of town and village development. The right of election was abolished by the movement in 1931 when the government appointed mayors and the Councils. The Institution was reinstated in 1943, only to be abolished once again in 1963 as a result of Turkish demands for separate Municipalities in the towns. Because of the Greek majority, the mayors of the towns were Greek throughout the British administration, with the exception of Lefka which was a purely Turkish village and had a Turkish mayor and municipal council.

Community and village authorities

The Idare Madjlis were kept under the same name for many years. In the end, however, they took on the character of communal and village authorities even though the members kept the Turkish titles, such as the Mukhtar or the president, the Aza, or the member. These titles are even used today by the people. The work of the village authorities was, and continues to be similar to the work of the Municipal Councils in the towns. The institution of electing these authorities was abolished in 1931, and from that time they were appointed.

Judiciary authority

The foundations of English justice were laid in 1881 by special decree which established a Supreme Court made up of the Chief Justice and two Judges; and the District Courts made up of a president and two deputy Judges, one Greek and one Turk. The chief justice, the judges of the supreme court and Presidents of the District Courts were all British. the same decree also established a Criminal Court, Magistrates Courts and police courts. In 1927, changes were introduced into the system allowing the appointment of natives to the position of presidents of District Courts. Under the same provisions natives could now also be appointed to the position of Attorney General and Counsel for the Crown. Related to the judiciary there were also the positions of the Interpreters, under a Chief Interpreter.

Security

The island's external security was the responsibility of the British government which maintained a small military contingent on the island, which could easily be strengthened from the fleet which was in the area. Command of this force was in the hands of the Grand Governor who also had the rank of Commander-in-chief. Internal security was in the hands of the Police Force in which the lower ranks and junior officers kept the Turkish titles of Zaptie, (constable), Chaoush, (seargent), and Mullazim, (officer). Rural constables were responsible for the protection of property in the countryside. They also kept the Turkish title of Turkopoullos. When in 1955 EOKA started its revolution, among other security measures the English also established the Auxiliary Police force with only Turks as members.

Economy policy We know that one of the conditions of the 1878 supplementary agreement was that British had to pay the Porte 93 thousand pounds. In order to meet this sum, as well as the money for the high salaries of the British government officials, the British not only kept the then existing taxation of the Turkish administration, but they also increased it, causing severe reaction from the population. The elected members of the House complained all the time but to no avail because the House had no right to amend the English salaries or the budget, since the Grand Governor had the veto. The only way they could do anything was to refuse to vote for the budget or for parts of the budget. This happened many times, but then it was enforced by Royal Decree. This struggle became even more intense after 1914. With the entry of Turkey into World War one on the side of Germany, the British made Cyprus a British possessions and continued to levy 43 thousand pounds in taxes, even though they stopped their payment to the Porte.

Mineral wealth farming industry Exploitation of natural resources and development of agriculture and industry fall within financial and economic policy. The British were successful in exploiting natural resources. By encouraging foreign company investments, the British got the rich mines of the island to produce once more. During Byzantine times the mines had been neglected but now they once again became the most basic product in support of the island's economy. In the agricultural sector one can credit the British with the introduction of new and different varieties of agricultural products and breeds of animals which were more productive. The slowness of efforts to enrich underground water resources, through construction of surface projects, however, resulted in frequent destruction of crops because of drought, a very frequent phenomenon in Cyprus. In the industrial sector the British administration showed a very limited interest. Despite the lack of protective legislation, the shoe and ready clothes industries did demonstrate noteworthy development.

Education policy Until 1895, when the law regulating all matters related to establishment of elementay schools was enacted, government interest was limited to the inspection of schools by an British inspector, and their subsidization on the basis of his report. School maintenance and the salaries of teachers were the repsosibility of the community and the Church. Frequent representations for responsible handling of education matters by the Government remained without result, because the Government insisted on its more active involvement in matters of appointments and the school programs, which were rejected by church and the island's political authorities. The church and political authorities saw in this government insistence a desire to Anglicize education, a thing which did take place later. The teachers, however, also insisted on this government involvement because their salaries, both for Greeks and Turks alike was very low. some Turkish teachers did not get more than six pounds per year, and some Greeks got only 15. Teachers also fell victim to political party confrontations. In 1923 when this indignation reached a climax the Greek members of the house and the government voted in the education law under which the government took all responsibility for appointment, transfers, retirement and salaries of elementary school teachers. As of that year education gradually fell into the hands of the government and was completed with the abolition of the Pancyprian teachers College in 1933 and establishment of intercommunal male and female colleges for the training of teachers and complete control of education under the laws of 1935 and 1952.

Illiberal measures of 1931   The fact that government policy aimed at disorienting education from what they considered a «national» education, at least in the case of the Greek inhabinants, and the cultivation of a colonial way of thinking, as it was always feared, can be seen by the illiberal measures adopted after the 1931 movement. Teaching of Greek history and geography was prohibited in the elementary schools. Also prohibited was the display in schools of pictures of the heroes of the Greek revolution, the use of the Greek national anthem and the Greek flag. This aimed at eradication of anything which connected Cypriot Hellenism with Greece. The government introduced the English language in the training of teachers in the Intercommunal teachers colleges, to the degree that teachers were inefficient in the Greek language. It lowered teachers qualifications in secondary schools which had accepted Government control to the degree that a graduate of a high school could teach the humanities if he earned the «Cyprus Certificate» in government examinations on these humanities. The schools which, for economic reasons, accepted the 1935 law were few and only one school accepted the provisions of the law of 1952. Thus secondary education to a great degree managed to remain independent.

Suppressive measures 1955-59   Illiberal measures against education became truly oppressive during the EOKA struggle of 1955-1959. The reason was that schools had a lively presence in that struggle during which both the teachers and students gave their lives. The expulsion of all professors from Greece was one such measure. This created a very serious teaching problem in the secondary education field because there were great numbers of such Greek teachers. A number of teachers who, according to the Inspector of Education were conducting a national policy, were not allowed to teach. Elementary schools that flew the Greek flag were closed for as long as they exhibited the Greek flag. Schools, the students of which took part in the student demonstrations, were taken off the roster of secondary education schools. A great number of such schools remained closed for long periods as a result of this measure.

English policy in other departments English policy in other Departments must be described as progressive. The Public Works Departments (P.W.D.) was extremely active right from the start. Expansion, improvement and surfacing of the road system so that towns were all connected with the villages, and development of domestic and foreign tourism are some of the characteristics of this policy. Maintenance of the old forests and reforestation, as well as protection of forests through construction of a wide network of forest roads and a large staff of forest rangers were the work of a progressive department of Forests. Establishment of hospitals in the towns and medical units in the villages and their staffing and equipment with specialists and diagnostic and other apparatus were equally progressive achievements of the Department of Heatlh. The strong and lively interest in ancient monuments and the suppression of grave-looting and the smuggling of antiques, exploration and excavation of ancient sites both by the Department of Antiquities, as well as encouragement of schools of archeology to conduct such excavations and research, demontrate a sincere desire to research Cyprus prehistory. All these policies are to the credit of the British administration. If, at the same time, the British administration had followed a more correct economic policy, with full exploitation of natural resources and the encouragement of industry, Cyprus could have become a very developed and wealthy country, as it has proved to be after its independence.

ENGLAND-TURKEY-GREECE-CYPRUS

Cyprus
possession, 1914
colony, 1925
From 1878 British paid 93 thousand pounds to Turkey until 1907 when this sum was cut by 50 thousand pounds. In 1914, when Turkey joined Germany in World War One, against British, the island was declared a British possession and all obligations towards Turkey ceased. The Cypriots, however, continued to be taxed in the amount of 43 thousand pounds untill 1917 when the tax was abolished. On 10 March 1925 Cyprus was declared a Crown Colony, and remained as such until 1960, which was the end of the British occupation.

Cypriots in the
Greek wars
It is a fact that the Cypriots welcomed the British to Cyprus, bearing in mind the British gesture on the Ionian islands, and they believed that their desire for Enosis, or union with Greece, would now be fulfilled. This desire was inborn and firm, because no conqueror was able to blunt this national sentiment with his passage through the island. The Cypriots always considered the wars of Greece as their own wars and for this reason they joined the ranks of the Greek armed forces voluntarily both during the Greek revolution and the war of 1897 - - despite an British prohibition of this, as well as during the Balkan Wars and during both World Wars in 1914 and 1939. They also volunteered for the Asia Minor campaign of 1921 to 22.

Cyprus offered
to Greece
The right of Cyprus to unite with Greece was recognized by many British politicians. They considered this desire very natural. Among them were Gladstone, Churchill, Lloyd George and others. It was, however, recognised more officially in 1915 when Cyprus was offered to Greece in exchange for Greece joining the war on the side of Britain and its allies. The offer was, however, rejected because of the differences between the Greek king of that time, Constantine, and Eleftherios Venizelos, which led the nation to adventures and anomalies, the results of which in the long term led in the Asia Minor disaster of 1922.

Lauzanne treaty and Enosis   The Treaty of Lauzanne was signed in 1923, and under it Turkey gave up all rights upon Cyprus. This led the Greeks in Cyprus to launch a strong campaign for Enosis. The subject was continually raised by the Greek members in the House and with memorandums and missions to London. One such mission was udertaken immediately upon the end of World War One in 1918, with Archbishop Cyril the third. The delegation stayed in the British capital until 1920, when it was reinforced with new enthusiastic members of the Legislative Council. It failed in its goal and the same fate followed a new mission in 1929. In their efforts to quel this desire for Enosis, the British used suppressive measures, one of which was to exile two of the patriots.

The 1931 movement   This took a different turn with the return of the 1929 mission from London. On 21 October 1931, and under the leadership of Bishop Mylonas of Kition, the Greek members of the House resigned en-masse, and with flaming speeches they called upon the people to rise with passive resistence. The residents of Nicosia gathered at the old women's market towards the end of the present Ledra street, and from there they marched to the Governor's residence to present him with a petition. Police intervened along the way in an effort to disperse the marchers. The first modern martyr of modern Cypriot liberty, Onoufrios Clerides died when he was hit by a bullet. In anger, the crowd then marched to Government House which they set on fire. The movement was, in the end suppressed both in Nicosia and other towns, where minor incidents took place the next day. The British then adopted harsher measures. They exiled the Metropolitan Bishops, Mylonas of Kition, and Makarios of Kyrenia, and Communal Leaders Dionysios Kykkotis, Anthonis Theodotou, Georgios Hadjipavlou, Nicolas Lanitis and Savvas Loizides. They also abolished all constitutional freedoms, they suppressed education, banned the use of bells in the churches, like the Turks had done in the past, and they ruled for long in a dictatorial manner and under decrees from the Governor.

Greek support   The voice of Enosis was sillenced under these measures and was only heard in secret in the secondary schools. The same did not happen in Greece, however. Although Eleftherios Venizelos was forced by developments to denounce the movement in the Greek parliament, the Greek people themselves expressed their support in many different ways, one of which was to form the Central Committee for the Cyprus Struggle by world prominent personalities, which kept the movement alive in Greece.

232

Revival of hopes   The suppressive measures in Cyprus did not manage to close the mouth of the people. Immediatetly after the start of World War Two the people launched another strong Enosis campaign. In this mew campaign the people were led by the belief that their just and moral claim lay within the goals for which free humanity was fighting together with Britain, and that for this very reason their claim would be satisfied. They also based their hopes on the assurances of Winston Churchill the Prime Minister of victory, to his Greek counterpart Emmanuell Tsouderos, that Britain would fulfill the national claims of Greece. It is characteristic that there was no British reaction when, at a dinner, Tsoudheros on 15 November 1941 in London, stressed in a toast: «I dream of a Grand Greece which will include Northern Epirus, the Dodecanese, Macedonia and Cyprus». The lack of British reaction was welcomed in Cyprus as a proof of British consent for the union of Cyprus with Greece.

New missions
1950 plebiscite   Hopes, however, were once again dashed. A national mission under the Locum Tenense of the Archepiscopal Throne, Leontios, returned to Cyprus in 1947, after a lengthy stay in Britain but brought no results. On 15 January 1950, Archbishop Makarios the Second conducted a plebiscite among the Greek residents of Cyprus in which 97 percent voted in support of Enosis. In the same year a second mission under the Metropolitan Bishop of Kyrenia Kyprianos toured Greece, Britain and the United States with the volumes of the plebiscite, but it also came back wihtout any result.

Makarios the
Third Mission   The resolution of the UN Social Committee of 17 December 1952, which recognised the right of the non-self-governig peoples to regulate their future through a plebiscite, and the declaration of Human Rights, which Britain also singed, revived the hopes of the Cypriot people for success. In 1953, Archbishop Makarios the Third visited the United States of America in order to lodge a Cyprus appeal before the United Nations, but once again there was no result.

Papagos
appeal 1954   The Cyprus issue started to get a new turn as of 1954. Until that time the Greek governments, in their effort to maintain good relations with Britain and in their effort to avoid any disruption of Western and NATO defence tried to stay far from the battle by stating that the Cyprus issue is a matter of interest to the Cypriot people and the British Government. A visit by Anthony Eden to Greece in early 1954, however, dissolved any delusions that

the Cyprus issue could be solved through peaceful means. This new fact was confirmed be the statement of Foreing undersecretary Hopkinson before parliament, that «the right of self determination will never be recognised for Cyprus». Greek Prime Minister Marshal Papagos then lodged on behalf of the Cypriot people an appeal with the United Nations, despite strong pressure from the United States to wait.

Reaction from Cyprus   Progress of this first Greek appeal was dramatic. both the British, as well as the Greek delegations used all their diplomacy, and when on 21 Sept., a vote was cast on whether to accept or reject the discussion of the appeal by the plenum of the United Nations, Greece won the vote with 30 votes for, 19 against, and 11 abstentions. After this success, Britain moved in every possible direction and convinced the United States to exert new pressure upon Greece to accept postponement of the discussion until the new General Assembly convened, in order to give Britain and Greece the time to examine the issue between them. Reaction to the postponement was very strong in the island. All Cypriot organizations, rightish and leftist in a joint declaration called upon the people to an all island general strike on 18 December. Large scale demonstrations in Nicosia and in Limassol were then dispersed by the army and the police. It became very clear from that moment on that the struggle was taking a new form, particularly after those demonstrations cost the life of two youths and left another paralysed.

EOKA struggle 1 Apr. 1955   In January 1955 the British had discovered a motorboat, Agios Georgios, off the coast of Paphos, loaded with arms and ammunition. The crew, all Greeks from Greece, with exiled Cypriot Socrates Loizides, were all arrested and sentenced to from 4 to 12 years in prison. Seven Cypriots from the village of Chloraka, found unloading the schooner were given from one to four years in prison. A proclamation from the National Organization for Cyrpiot Struggle, EOKA, over the signature of the «Leader Dhigenis», warned the people that the struggle would be armed and called for the peoples collaboration. On 1st of April, Cyprus was steeped in darkness and explosions rocked Nicosia, Larnaca and Limassol. The struggle had begun.

Tripartite conference   The time for the UN General Assembly session was approaching but there was no contact between the English and the Greek governments in accordance with the assembly's resolution on the postponement, and for this reason the Greek government was preparing to lodge a new appeal. This fact wor-

234

ried the Eden government, which thought up a diplomatic manoeuvre and the Greek government fell into the trap. This brought on even more adverse consequences for the Cyprus issue. Under the allegation that Turkey also had interests in Cyprus the Eden government called for a tripartite - Britain, Greece, Turkey, conference in London, to discuss the fate of the Cypriot people who were not even represented. It remains a fact that the negative results of the conference did lead Greece to lodge a new appeal, but its acceptance to sit at a meeting together with Turkey, was a great diplomatic error, because in this way it recognised for Turkey the right to have a say in the Cyprus issue, while the matter was purely a matter of self-determination. Britain exploited this diplomatic error and managed to have the General Assembly not to discuss the Greek appeal.

Proclamation of wanted persons, detentions without trial   Throughout this period the activities of EOKA were mounting. The governor of Cyprus, Sir Walter Armitage was nearly killed on 24 May, when a bomb placed under his seat in a cinema exploded only minutes after his departure. Rewards reaching upto five thousand pounds for EOKA's deputy chief and 10 thousand pounds for Grivas Dhigenis were posted, but they brought no results. There was no result in efforts to bend the peoples will when the notorious personal detention law was enacted on 15 July 1955. This law gave the right to the government to declare anyone as a terrorist and have him locked up without trial. Under this law which remained in effect until 1959, some thousands of Cypriots were held in various detention camps. The largest mass detention under this law occurred on 21 July 1958, when under a house curfew some 1,600 people were arrested.

Harding - Makarios meeting   Chief of the Imperial General Staff, Field Marshall John Harding took over as governor of the island on 3 October 1955. Appointment of a milittary person as governor, meant that the British government was determined to suppress the armed struggle and enforce a solution drawn up by the Foreing secretary, Harold McMillan, and which had been rejected at the tripartite conference in London. Wanting to have a negotiation for a peaceful solution, Harding invited Archbishop Makarios the Third to a meeting at the «Ledra Palace» Hotel on the day after his arrival. At this meeting Makarios submitted three points: 1- Great Britain should recognise the right of self-determination for the people of Cyprus. 2- After this recognition the Greeks would cooperate in the drafting of a constitution. 3- The time for the implementation of self-determination must be discussed with the Greeks to be elected on the basis of the Cyprus constitu-

Commander Dhigenis with his staff in accordance to a photograph found in his hide-out, during a search in Paphos forest in June 1956.

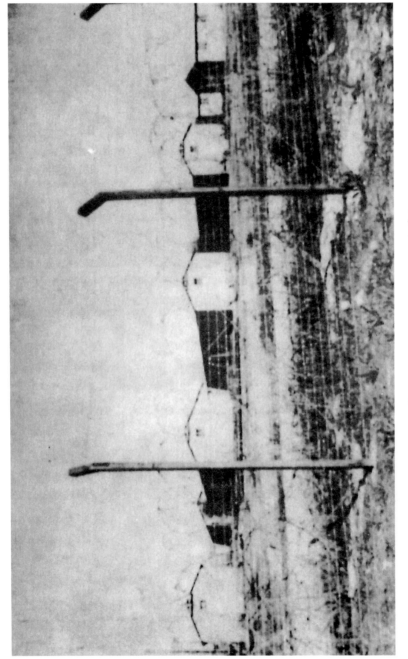

The personal detention law came into force on 15 July 1955. More than four thousand people incarcerated in detention and other camps under this law. Pictured is the Kokkinotrimithia detention camp.

tion. The proposed points were passed on by Harding to the British government, and when the next meeting was held three days later, it became clear that its intention was to enforce the McMillan plan.

State of
Emergency

A long time, however, went by before a new meeting was held and in the time between and as a result of increased EOKA actions, Harding declared a state of emergency on the island on 27 November 1955 and on the same day he published regulations which gave him unlimited authorities.

Makarios and his
aids in exile

When the Harding - Makarios talks were resumed in early 1956, the government was unwilling to grant a general amnesty as a start to the talks, and this made finding a solution even more difficult. Brirish Colonial Secretary Alan Lennox Boyd arrived in Cyprus at the end of February but talks with him also remained without any result. When the deadlock became final, Harding, in following his harsh policy, arrested the Archbishop and Bishop of Kyrenia Kyprianos, the Phaneromeni chief priest Papastavros Papagathangelou and the secretary of Kyrenia Bishopric Polykarpos Ioannides. On 9 March 1956 they were all exiled to San Sousi on Mahe Island of the Seychelles group.

Reaction in
Cyprus and
Greece

Reaction to the Archbishop's arrest and exile were particularly strong. EOKA intensified its activities to the degree that it caused concern and confusion to Harding, who mobilised every possible means at his disposal in an effort to find and arrest George Grivas, the leader Dhigenis. Some five thousand troops combed the Paphos forest in June 1956, on some information that he was hiding there. The result was negative. Reaction in Greece was even stronger. The Greek ambassador in London was immediately recalled and a new appeal was lodged at the United Nations. A communique after a Greek cabinet meeting condemned the British action as an «act incompatible with the civilization of our times» and as an act «directed against the head of one of the most ancient churches of Christendom».

The English lose
their cool

As expected, under the pressure of developements on the island, Harding and his advisors lost their cool head. There can be no other explanation for their barbaric behaviour in the case of Grigoris Afxendiou. Being unable to capture him while he fought them single handed from his hide-out in a cave near Macheras Monastery, they burned him alive on 3 March

238

1957. Similarly there is no other explanation for the same act against the four heroes of Liopetri and Kyriakos Matsis in his hide-out at Dhikomo village. There is no other explanation either for their Medieval tortures methods used against detainees, even on children, by re-introducing the punishment of flogging. There can be no other explanation for the mass punishment of entire villages like the curfews which went on for days. A curfew at Milikouri village went on for 54 days, and gave rise to a Council of Europe investigation into the violation of human rights.

Radcliffe constitution These inhuman and barbaric measures at long last touched the emotions of the civilized world, and of Britain itself, when the government, in an effort to minimize impressions, and under pressure from the Labour opposition, it sent world famous constitutional expert Radcliffe to Cyprus with a mandate to study the situation and submit a liberal self-government constitution which was to be presented to the interested parties. This constitution was rejected by the Greek government, and by Makarios himself when it was taken to the Seychelles for his consideration.

UN resolution inmates set free 28 Mar. 1957 The Greek appeal was discussed by the UN General Assembly on 18 February 1957 and a resolution was unanimously approved expressing the wish for a peaceful solution, and a just one in accordance with the principles of the UN Constitutional Charter. This was considered satisfactory by the Greek government. In a proclamation a few days later EOKA declared it would abide with the spirit of the UN resolution, and would cease all operations as soon as the exiled Archbishop Makarios was set free. Under the pressure of developments the British government allowed the exiles to leave the Seychelles and settle in Athens, March-April 1957. This act was interpreted in Cyprus and in Greece as a sincere desire of the Macmillan government to solve the Cyprus issue in a just way.

Partition central British idea This was not so simple. From the moment that the British got Turkey involved in the Cyprus issue, through the tripartite conference in London, Turkish demands started to increase under British encouragement. It was England which dropped officially, the idea of partition of the island in a statement of Colonial Secretary Lennox Boyd on 19 December 1956. He told Parliament that if the Greeks got the right for self-determination, then the same right should be given to the Turks. The idea of partition was expressed even more clearly in the Macmillan plan which provided for the administrative division of the island for seven years, and then a joint sovereignty by Britain, Greece, and Turkey.

Turkish atrocities   The Macmillan plan was, naturally, rejected both by the Archbishop and by Greece. Turkey, however, accepted it, and this helped British diplomacy to apply greater pressures in an effort to force its unilateral implementation. This blackmail also had a second origin. In its effort to convince the world that the co-existence of Greeks and Turks was impossible on the island, Britain, insisting that partition was the only solution, did encourage the leaders of the Turkish Cypriots to commit atrocities against the Greeks, hoping that this would turn EOKA against the Turks in reprisals. 1958 is now considered the year of the start of grievous events between the two communities, with the massacre at Gionelli on 12 June 1958 as the climax. During this incident, eight youths from the village of Kondemenos who had been arrested by the British, were set free in the purely Turkish village Gionelly, so that they could walk back to their own village. They were all massacred by the Turks only minutes after the British left. During the four years of the EOKA struggle, a total of 68 Greeks were massacred by the Turks, and of these, 61 died between June and October 1958.

Zurich accords 11   While the struggle continued with undiminished
Feb. 1959   tension, on 17 Sept. 1958 the UN General Assembly resolved to once again discuss the Greek appeal lodged after the failure of the talks between the Greek government and British Prime Minister Macmillan in London in the presence of the new governor of Cyprus Sir Hugh Foot. In view of this debate, Britain undertook a broad diplomatic campaign, while contacts were going on between England, Greece, and Turkey, towards finding a solution. These talks ended in a Zurich meeting of the Prime Ministers and Foreign Ministers of the three countries on 11 Feb. 1959 at which was signed by the communal leaders Archbishop Makarios and Fazil Kuchuk.

Agreement   The delegations arrived in London after many
ratification in meetings and excessive pressures upon Archbishop
London   Makarios both from the British and the Greek sides, forced him to sign the ratification of the Zurich agreements on 19 Feb. 1959. The Representative of the Turkish Cypriots, Dr. Fazil Kuchuk also ratified the accord. Hostilities officially ended as of that date.

Under the Zurich and London agreements the British colonial regime

The mausolium of Ethno-Martyr Kyprianos and the Metropolitan Bishops of Paphos, Kition, and of Kerynia who were massacred on 9 July 1821. It is in the courtyard of Phaneromeni Church in Nicosia.

The monument to the fighters of EOKA on the old ramparts of Nicosia near the Archbishopric. Both monuments testify to the sacrifices of the Cypriot people in their struggle to win independence for Cyprus.

This monument was erected by the people of Kerynia over the hide-out of Kyriakos Matsis, to remind us and coming generations of the dedication of this golden-eagle hero of the Pendadaktylos range, and of the courage of his personal sacrifice. His reply to the British, who called on him surrender was: "If I come out I come fighting." His father is here pictured laying a wreath at the monument´s inauguration in January 1961, by Archbishop Makarios.

**Main
provisions of
the agreements**
came to an end and the Republic of Cyprus was established. Britain maintained the right to keep military
bases on the island. Administration entered a part-
nership basis between the Greeks and Turks of the
island in a manner not in conformity with the population ratio of the two island communities. Employment in government service and the police was
to be on the basis of 70 to 30 percent and in the army on a 60:40 ratio
and this despite the fact that the population ratio was 80 percent Greeks
to 18 percent Turks. The agreements also provided for the division of the
municipalities in the town of Nicosia, Limassol, Famagusta, Larnaca and
Paphos. In addition to the House of Representatives there would be two
Communal Houses, one each for the two communities responsible for
handling communal religious, educational and cultural affairs of each
community. Under the agreements the President is always Greek and the
Vice President Turkish. The Turks were given three of the ten Ministries,
and they had 15 of the 50 seats in the House of Representatives. The
Speaker of the House was always Greek, and his Assistant Speaker a
Turk. Voting was universal and decisions were taken by majority, with the
exception of matters of custom laws, the budget law where separate voting and separate majority was needed. This demonstrates the trend for
administrative division and partition which always remains the British aim.

A Treaty of guarantee was signed between Britain, Greece and Tur-
**Treaty of
Guarantee**
key, in order to guarantee the independence and integrity of the Republic of Cyprus. This Treaty was an
integral part of the Zurich and London agreements.
Under this treaty the three powers have the right to intervene, either joint-
ly, or each one separately to remove any danger to the independence
and integrity of Cyprus. In the implementation of this clause it was agreed
that a Greek force, (EL.DY.K) of 1200 men and a Turkish force
(TUR.DY.K) of 800 men would be stationed on the island. Long discussions were held in London over this treaty because Makarios considered
that foreign powers were given the right to interfere with Cyprus domestic
and other affairs, an independent and sovereign state in violation to the
basic principles of the UN Constitutional Charter. It is this treaty which
gave the Turks the right to invade on 20 July 1974 and to occupy 40 percent of the territory of Cyprus, instead of protecting the independence
and integrity of the Republic as the treaty provides.

**Makarios
returns
1 Mar. 1959**
With the signing of the agreements the exile of
Archbishop Makarios became null and void. Makarios
was the first to return to the island on 1 March 1959

243

receiving a grand welcome from some 250 thousand people from all over the island. Leader Dighenis, however, was absent from this grand welcome, because the British had not allowed him even to leave his hide-out. All the other wanted men were given an amnesty, and they paraded before the Archbishop in a touching development of that grand day.

The agreements and Digenis
The solution given was not the one that Cypriot Hellenism desired and fought for. In an effort not to cause the division of the people, Leader Deghenis did accept it and on 9 March in a proclamation he underlined that instead of a war song he was proclaiming concord, unity and love in order to erect the new young Republic from the ashes of the Cypriot epic. When, according to the British provisions he left the island on 15 March, he called upon the people to unite around Ethnarch Makarios who remained the symbol of unity and of strength. His return to Greece was triumphal. The people accorded him a grand welcome and the government heaped honours upon him.

First election for president
The Interval between the return of Makarios and establishment of the Republic was devoted by Sir Hugh Foot to consultations with the Archbishop and Dr. Kuchuk on solving problems which could naturally arise from implementation of the accords. To give authority to the consultations the Governor then proclaimed the first Presidential elections. On 13 December Archbishop and Ethnarch Makarios was elected the first President of Cyprus and Dr. Fazil Kuchuk was elected Vice President.

British bases
The area to be covered by the British bases on the island, was the subject discussed the longest, and the tone often endangered the agreements themselves. In the end the matter was settled in accordance with the President's wish that no Greek villages should be incorporated within the bases. Two British bases were established, one at Dhekelia and the second at Episkopi - Akrotiriu.

Constitution
Great obstacles and difficulties were also met in the preparation of the Constitution of Cyprus. The task was entrusted to prominent constitutional experts, Athens University Professor Themistocles Tsatsos who acted as chairman, and Ankara University professor Nihat Erim, Glavcos Clerides representing the Greeks and Rauf Denktash representing the Turkish Cypriots.

Unresolved issues One of the most serious obstacles was the matter of separate municipalities. This, in the end, was left to be dealt with by the two Communal Chambers, so that the constitution could function. In December 1963, the Turkish members of the House of Representatives cited this unresolved matter of the municipalities in order to refuse to ratify tax laws and the 1964 budget. In the end Makarios signed these laws, and the act was described as unconstitutional by the Turks, while the President argued that the state must go on functioning. This rift led to the events of 21 December which have the present tragedy as their sequel. Another unresolved matter was employment in public service with the 70:30 ratio. In order to hire Turkish Cypriots, it was necessary to dismiss many Greeks and hire Turks in their stead. This was unconstitutional. The other solution was to hire supernumeraries, and this would have degraded public service. This was understood by the Turks who agreed with a gradual implementation of the provision.

First parliamentary elections The first elections for members of the House of Representatives were held on 31 July 1960. Members of the Communal Chambers were elected on 7 August. The talks for settling all unresolved matters, with the exception of the two mentioned above, ended on the day before the Communal Chamber elections, and the agreements and 83 other documents were initialled at Government House. At midnight of the 15th to the 16th of August 1960 the Governor of Cyprus, Sir Hugh Foot recognised the independence of Cyprus, by reading a decree from Queen Elizabeth in the House of Representatives, by which the British era in Cyprus came to an end. The official declaration of the Republic took place at noon on 16 August in the same hall of the House of Representatives, and the President and Vice President gave their oath of allegiance to the constitution of Cyprus, and the Republic came into being.

THE INDEPENDENT REPUBLIC OF CYPRUS

Membership in the UN and the Commonwealth After a period of continual slavery lasting 769 years, Cyprus found itself in the company of independent states as of noon on 16 August 1960. The island was now prepared to work hard in order to rebuild the ruins bequeathed to it by the four-year struggle, and to play its part as a country devoted to the ideals of liberty for which it had fought and worked so hard. To confirm this ideal, the Government's first act was to request membership in the United Nations Organization. This was done on 20 September 1960 and the island was recognised as a State equal to all the other Member States. Five months later, on 16 February 1961, the British Parliament accepted the application of Cyprus for membership in the Commonwealth, a fact which provided Cyprus with economic benefits as well as cultural exchanges, both so important in its first steps.

The first cabinet The above steps were the result of correct evaluations and the political handling of the President and the members of the government who were determined, right from the start, to proceed with speedy restoration. The first Ministerial Cabinet was sworn in before the President on the same day as the declaration and the establishment of the Republic on 16 August 1960. There were ten Minutries: Foreign Affairs, Finance, Interior, Labour and Social Insurance, Commerce and Industry, Justice, Communications and Works, Defence, Agriculture, and Health.

Economic Social and cultural progress This start augured a bright future and progress during the first years. It was truly phenomenal in the economic, social and cultural fields. Rain water was conserved by dams in the most suitable sites. This increased cultivated lands and increased the agricultural production to the degree that agrarian exports revitalised the economy. The encouragement of capital for establishing industrial units not only contributed to a cut in imports, but it also increased the export of industrial products.

One of the first steps of the Greek Communal Assembly of Cyprus, was to strengthen technical and professional training. It achieved this by founding technical and professional schools, spending towards this end, the entire grant in subsidies from the Greek government. Above: The Technical School of Famagusta and below the Technical School of Xeros. They are now under Turkish occupation.

Pictured above is the Technical School of Nicosia. The Assembly took it over from the British and completed it in such a manner that it rose to today´s high level of technical education. Below:

The Severios Elementary School of Kerynia which, with additions provided by the Assembly, was turned into a Technical School. It is now under Turkish occupation.

Many facilities offered to businessmen for establishing hotel units throughout the island, utilization of the antiquities sites and the island's beauty areas, the straightening and widening of the road system, efforts of tourism which became one of the main and most profitable industries. Adoption of the Social Insurance law made the island a pioneer in social justice and the rise of trade unionism and the cooperative movement cut nearly all trends at profiteering and exploitation. The activities of the Communal Chambers, particularly of the Greek chamber, with its attention to the teaching profession and the establishment of technical as well as professional education and training, gave an unprecedented push, with the help of the people of the arts and of learning, to cultural and spiritual development. At the same time, the cultivation of close ties between Greece for the Greeks and Turkey for the Turks went to underline their determination to make the island prosper without sacrificing their individual ethnic origins.

Makarios and amendment of the constitution
While everything showed that very soon Cyprus would be joining the ranks of the fast developing countries, we have the apperance of the first constitutional complications which arose because of the divisive elements in the Zurich and London agreements. As pointed out earlier, the thorniest problem was that of the division of the municipalities. Discussions for a way out continued for three years, but no solution was found. In an effort to force a solution, the Turks used the right of veto of the the Vice President, with the Turkish Members of the House refusing to vote on customs and tax laws which required separate majorities of the Greeks and Turks in the House. Seeing that the state could not function in this manner, the President sent a document to the UN Secretary General requesting 13 amendments to the constitution. He also stated at the same time that if the Turks refused the amendments, he would go ahead in implementing them unilaterally.

Hostilities and a Security Council resolution
The reaction of the Turks, both in Cyprus and in Turkey was so severe that it led to first a small clash on 21 December 1963, which later spread. Nicosia, Limassol, Paphos and Kyrenia were shaken by bloody clashes and Cyprus found itself divided into two camps ready to annihilate each other. The situation was tragic. When Turkey threatened with an invasion under the excuse of protecting the constitution, as provided for under the Treaty of Guarantee, the Cyprus government appealed to the UN Security Council. In a resolution on 4 March 1964 the Council called on UN Member States to abstein from any act which could

The Presidential Palace as it was before the invasion. It fostered all hopes for a more prosperous future following abolition of the colonial regime by Archbishop and Ethnarch Makarios.

The curse of dissention, which has caused so many of the calamities of the Greek nation, completed its task in the ruins of the Presidential Palace from which Ethnarch Makarios fought to curb dissention by the Turks.

be considered an interindependence and integrity. The same resolution requested the government, recognised as the sole legal authority on the island, for permission to establish a peace keeping force on the island. This was done and the peace keeping force continues to remain on the island.

Security Council resolution 22 Dec. 1967

Even after this first resolution the clashes continued on the island reaching a climax with the battle of Saint Hilarion on 25 April 1964 and the battle of Mansoura-Kokkina on 7 to 9 August 1964, which resulted in the fall of many Turkish defence positions. The Turkish airforce then intervened and using Napalm bombs it set fire to and destroyed villages in the Tylliria area. Turkey also threatened with invasion, which however, was prevented with the intervention of the United States and Russia. The invasion threat was repeated with greater force in November 1967, when General George Grivas, who commanded the National Guard carried out an attack on Kophinou and Agios Theodoros as a result of ambushes set up by the Turks along the Nicosia-Limassol highway. This operation nearly led to a Greek-Turkish war which was averted through the intervention of Cyrus Vance, and it ended in the withdrawal of all Greek forces - one brigade - which had been stationed in the island since 1964. UN Secretary General U-Thant also worked hard to prevent a Greek-Turkish war and he called the governments of Greece, Turkey and Cyprus to cooperate with him in restoring peace on the island. Responding to U-Thant's appeal the Cyprus government agreed to negotiate with the Turkish community on ways to solve the crisis and restore constitutional order. This was the start of the intercommunal talks between Glafcos Clerides representing the Greek side and Rauf Denktash representing the Turkish side. These talks, with lengthy recesses, continued until 1974 without showing points of contact.

The Junta and the 15 July 74 coup

The military government (the Junta) of Greece, which abolished the Greek government in a coup on 21 April, 1967, was considered responsible for the battle of Kophinou and the withdrawal of the Greek brigade. Its very intervention in Cyprus affairs was scandalous, and in every possible way it wanted to neutralise President Makarios and wipe him out because he opposed its own partitionist plans for Cyprus. It tried to eradicate the President many times. Under the incitement of its ambassador in Nicosia it encouraged the Bishops to dethrone Makarios. The result that there was a mutual dethronement. George Grivas arrived on the island under the initiative of the Junta and he set up EOKA B, which delivered unprecedented blows against the island's security and which, with its general behaviour managed to divide Cypriot Hellenism. When this division was accomplished, it undertook the 15 July 1974 coup against Cyprus, which is considered the greatest act of treason in Cypriot history. In the coup it tried to strike at, and eliminate the Ethnarch of the Cypriot people who was fighting to save the island from Turkey's partitionist and expansionist aspirations on Cyprus.

Turkish Invasion 20 Jul. 74 It is very questionable if, on a world-wide historic scale, any other coup ever had the tragic and calamitous results that the Cyprus coup achieved. Apart from the hundreds of dead and wounded, and the abolition of democratic institutions, it encouraged the Turkish government of Bulent Ecevit to invade Cyprus under the excuse of the Treaty of Guarantee and its duty to protect the Turkish Cypriots and restore constitutional law and order. The invasion took place on 20 July from a beach West of Kyrenia. After a severe bombing by air and shelling from the sea, Turkish troops landed, while at the same time hundreds of Turkish paratroopers landed in order to capture the camp of the Greek army forces and Nicosia airport. They failed in both. Despite the criminal unpreparedness of defences, the resistence of the defenders of Cyprus was such that even three days after the invasion the Turks were not able to establish a bridgehead on the beach. The National Guard, at the same time, neutralised the moves by the Turkish Cypriots in the towns and villages and tried to capture the strong points of Saint Hilarion in a two-pronged advance from Bella Pais and Prophet Elias. After repeated meetings of the Security Council the two sides accepted a cease fire at four in the afternoon of 22 July. At that point the Turks held - only a small area from the Porfyris' Beach area to Ayios Yeoryios. It was only after hostilities ceased, that they moved in violation of the cease fire towards Kyrenia, which they found undefended, occupied it, and moved furhter East to the Pakhyammos locality.

Completion of the invasion 14 Aug. 74 The invasion of Cyprus also ended the Greek Junta which was forced to give in to a civilian government with Constantinos Karamanlis as Prime Minister. He returned to Athens on 24 July to face a true chaos in which any help for Cyprus was a total impossibility. For this reason he responded to resolution 353 of 20 July under which the Security Council called on Greece, Turkey and Great Britain, in their capacity as guarantor powers, to negotiate, and he accepted such negotiations. It was agreed that the talks should be expanded with the participation of

The Archbishop's Palace cost hundreds of thousands of pounds and as a centre of culture, it presented the drive and vitality of our people internationally. The cracks visible, are like wounds in our own flesh inflicted by our very own enmities and disagreements. When will we ever be able to uproot this curse of our own race?

254

the two communities and with observers from Russia and the United States. This second round of talks was held in Vienna on 11 August. The demands of the Turks, however, were so lacking in logic that Greek Foreign Minister George Mavros and Glafcos Clerides were forced to withdraw. At that time Clerides was Acting President of the Republic of Cyprus. This was on 14 August, and the new and second cycle of Turkish opetations commenced a few hours later. In this new cycle of operations which the Security Council tried to stop in vain, the Turks used 40 thousand troops equipped with modern arms and equipment, and 200 tanks under continual air cover. They spread destruction everywhere. They stopped only when they achieved their goal with the conquest of 40 percent of Cyprus territory which included the most fertile parts of the Mesaoria and Karpass plains, the district of Morphou and Lapithos, as well as most tourist areas of the island in Kyrenia and in Famagusta.

Account of calamities from the invasion

The victims of the invasion in battle dead, massacred, people executed in cold blood, raped women, amount to some two thousand. In addition there are 1619 missing persons whose fate remains unknown to this day. In addition to these, another 200 thousand people were chased out of their homes, living as refugees in their own country, having lost their property and far from the graves of their forefathers. There are also hundreds of people who live enclaved in the Karpass area at the invaders mercy. To all this one must add the resurrected institution of Turkish colonization which is exclusively aimed at altering the demographic character of the island. This sums up an evaluation of the calamities caused by the tragedy of the treasonous coup and the barbaric invasion which followed it.

General Assembly resolution 3212 Security Council resolution 365

Cypriot Hellenism looked for its salvation in Archbishop Makarios who survived the coup and he returned to the island on 6 Dec. He immediately commenced a strong campaign and managed to move the entire free world with his plea and also managed to win the battle at the General Assembly of the United Nations with its unanimous resolution 3212 of 1 November 1974 it:

1. Called on all states to respect the sovereignty indepencence, territorial integrity and non-aligned character of the Republic of Cyprus and to abstein from any acts or intervention against it.

2. Requested the urgent withdrawal of all foreign troops from the Cyprus Republic and an end to all foreign intervention in its affairs.

3. It considered that the constitutional status of the Republic was the

Before July 20 1974, the people in these tents had lived in happiness in their own wealthy homes. Today they are still refugees, chased out of their homes and properties by Turkish Attila who continues to trample upon their human rights. There are 200 thousand such refugees waiting for their return home.

responsibility of the Greek and the Turkish Cypriot communities.

4. Recommended the start of contacts and talks on an equal basis, under the good offices of the UN Secretary General, between representatives of the two communities, and called for their continuation so that they could freely reach a political settlement which will be mutually acceptable and based on their fundamental and legal rights.

5. It considered that all refugees must return to their homes in security, and called upon the interested parties to take urgent steps towards this end.

6. It expressed the hope that if it became necessary, increased efforts, including talks, could be conducted within the United Nations for the purpose of implementing the provisions of the resolution, in a manner which will guarantee the right of independence, sovereignty, and territorial integrity of the Republic of Cyprus.

7. It requested the Secretary General to continue to furnish to all members of the population of Cyprus the humanitarian aid of the United Nations and it called on all states to contribute to this aid.

8. It called on the two sides to continue to cooperate completely with the peace keeping force which could be strengthened if the need arose.

9. Called on the Secretary General to continue to offer his good services to the interested parties.

This resolution, which is also so emphatic in its basis, was discussed by the UN Security Council on 13 December 1974 and it was also adopted under resolution 365 of the Security Council. General Assembly resolution 3212 became the basis for talks between the two communities which continued, with lenghthy recesses until 1977 without reaching any conclusion. Optimism was created after two meetings between Makarios and Rauf Denktash, on 27 January and 14 February 1977 - the second in the presence of UN Secretary General Kurt Waldheim - and after the constructive, as it was believed at that time, mission of presidental envoy Clark Clifford, after his tour of Athens, Ankara and Nicosia. When talks were resumed in Vienna, however, on 1 April 1977 the proposals of the Turkish Cypriot side were so far apart from what was agreed between Makarios and Denktash at their second meeting on 14 February, that all effort to continue the talks was abandoned, since it became clear that the Turks were only interested in maintaining the status quo.

Intercommunal talks   On the basis of the UN resolution, UN Secretary General Kurt Waldheim called upon the two sides to come to talks for a solution of their numerous differences on settlement of the Cyprus problem. Interlocutors Glafcos Cle-

The tragedy did not bring Cyprus to it's knees. It fought with courage to wipe out suffering and heal the wounds of the displaced people, by creating the prerequisites for the prevalence of justice. It placed it's displaced people in such housing estates which were built with the help of foreigners who felt its pain and tragedy, and offered generously towards reconstruction.

rides and Rauf Denktash had five meetings in Vienna during 1975 and 1976 in the presence of the Secretary General. They reached no agreement. The Turkish side insisted to ignore the UN resolutions dealing with the return of refugees, on property, and related matters.

Makarios-Denktash Seeing the deadlock, Archbishop Makarios ac-
summit cepted an invitation from Rauf Denktash to meet in
agreement order to discuss a framework for a solution of their differences. Two meetings were held, one on 27 January in the presence of the Secretary General's special representative in Cyprus and one on 12 February 1977 in the presence of the Secretary General himself. Results were deemed encouraging.

Following is the text of the agreement concluded on 12 February 1977:
1. We are seeking an independent, non-aligned, bi-communal Federal Republic.
2. The territory under the administration of each community should be discussed in the light of economic viability, of productivity and land ownership.
3. Questions like principles of freedom of movement, freedom of settlement, the right of property, and other specific matters, are open for discussions, taking into consideration the fundamental basis of a bi-communal federal system, and certain principal difficulties which may arise for the Turkish Cypriot Community.
4. The powers and functions of the central federal government will be such as to safeguard the unity of the country and having regard to the bi-communal character of the State.

Sixth round of Intercommunal talks were resumed on the basis
intercommunal and result of the summit accord of 12 February
talks 1977. The two sides did meet again in Vienna on 31 March and on 7 of April 1977. The Greek delegation came to the talks fully prepared and with complete proposals both on the return of lands, as well as on the constitution. But Rauf Denktash reneged from his summit agreement with Makarios, and undermined this new attempt.

Makarios dead, Talks were discontinued on 7 April and they were
3 Aug. 1977 not resumed through the whole of 1977. The first symptoms of cardiac irregularity for Makarios appeared at this period. In the end he succumbed on 3 August 1977 only a

few days after the greatest mass gathering ever held in Eleftheria Square in Nicosia, to condemn the coup and the Turkish invasion. Makarios' death came at the most critical juncture of the Cyprus issue.

Spyros Kyprianou succeeds Makarios   On the basis of the constitution the President is replaced by the Speaker of the House of Representatives. Thus under this provision Makarios was succeeded by Spyros Kyprianou on a temporary basis, and until regular presidential elections could be held. He did become the President after such an election, in which he was unopposed.

Kyprianou -Denktash summit   All attempts by the UN and the Secretary General to bridge the gap between the two communities through talks, came up against the unacceptable demands of the Turkish Cypriots. In an effort to lift the deadlock, the secretary general arranged a meeting between Kyprianou and Denktash which did take place on 18 and 19 May 1979. It ended in an agreement on ten points which did confirm the Makarios-Denktash summit agreement of February 1977.

Following is the text of the agreement:

1. It was agreed to resume intercommunal talks on 15 June 1979.

2. The basis for the talks will be the Makarios-Denktash guidelines of 12 February 1977 and the UN resolution relevant to the Cyprus question.

3. There should be respect for human rights and fundamental freedoms of all citizens of the Republic.

4. The talks will deal with all territorial and constitutional aspects.

5. Priority will be given to reaching an agreement on the settlement of Varosha under UN auspices, simultaneously with the beginning of the consideration by the interlocutors of the constitutional and territorial aspects of a comprehensive settlement. After agreement on Varosha has been reached, it will be implemented without waiting the outcome of the discussion on other aspects of the Cyprus problem.

6. It was agreed to abstein from any action which might jeopardize the outcome of the talks, and special importance will be given to initial practical measures by both sides to promote goodwill, mutual confidence and the return to normal conditions.

7. The demilitarization of the Republic of Cyprus is envisaged, and matters relating thereto will be discussed.

8. The independence, sovereignty, territorial integrity and the nonalignment of the Republic should be adequately guaranteed against union in whole or in part with any other country and against any form of partition or secession.

9. The intercommunal talks will be carried out in a continuing and sustained manner, avoiding any delay.

10. The intercommunal talks will take place in Nicosia.

Start of the talks   It was agreed that talks would start on 17 June 1979, but nothing happened. The Turkish Cypriot leader Denktash now demanded that before talks do start, the term "bicommunal" should be replaced by the term "bizonal." This was rejected by the Greek Cypriot side because acceptance of the term "bizonal" would basically mean partition of the island. Denktash also refused to have any discussion on the settlement of Varosha by its inhabitants under UN auspices. His excuse was that an appeal was pending in the courts involving Greek properties which allegedly belong to the Turkish organization Evkaf. Talks which resumed from time to time in 1980 and 1981 also ended in a fiasco. The Turkish Cypriots continued to insist that two separate states must be created. Under such a condition the Greek Cypriots would have no say in the administration of the Turkish state, while the Greek Cypriot state would be under Turkish Cypriot control via the figurative central government.

Demographic changes   The aim of the Turkish Cypriots and of Turkey itself to turn Northern Cyprus into a purely Turkish state can be seen through their joint efforts to settle Turks from Anatolia in Northern Cyprus. These efforts have taken on alarming proportions, since, fundamentally, the demographic character of the occupied areas was changing from its foundations. It is indicated by estimates that from the beginning of this colonization todate, some 75 thousand such colonists have been settled in Northern Cyprus. Many Turkish Cypriots were expatriated as a result of this influx of colonists. Worst was to come, however, when the Turkish Cypriot administration, in July 1982, began to give title deeds to both the Turkish Cypriots and to the colonists who had been settled on Greek properties. This also prejudged the Turkish Cypriot intent not to permit the return of the rightful owners to their homes and properties. This would, naturally, make a solution to the refugee problem even more complex and difficult. It is for these very reasons that President Kyprianou, in 1983, appealed to the UN General Assembly, thus internationalising the Cyprus issue.

UN General Assembly resolution of 13 May 1983   The General Assembly issued a strong resolution introduced by the non-aligned movement and supported by another 12 countries, made up of 17 articles. Of these, article seven and article eight, are

261

extremely definitive. Article seven considers the withdrawal of all occupation forces from Cyprus as an essential basis for a speedy and acceptable solution. Article eight asks for the immediate withdrawal of all occupation forces. Articles two and three are also very important. Article two recognizes the Government of the Republic as the only Government of the entire island, and article three condemns the issue of such title deeds to the Turkish Cypriots and the colonists, for holding Greek Cypriot properties.

Turkish reaction   Turkish Cypriot reaction was very direct and immediate. The Turkish Cypriot Legislative Assembly met on 17 June 1983, rejected the UN resolution and specifically the part that recognized only one legal Government. The assembly also ruled that the Turkish Cypriots have the very exclusive right to self-goverment (self administration) and they have the right to administration themselves as they wish.

Independent Turkish Cypriot State of Northern Cyprus   Both the Cyprus government and the UN Secretary General were very gravely concerned. The Secretary General tried to convince both sides to come to negotiations, with very specific proposals on all aspects of the Cyprus issue, territorial as well as constitutional. When his efforts failed, the Secretary General called on President Kyprianou and Rauf Denktash to a summit meeting, hoping that common ground could be found. He sent his Special representative, Hugo Gobbi, to Cyprus on 14 November 1983. He handed to the two leaders a letter from the Secretary General establishing a program for discussions. Instead of replying, Rauf Denktash on that very same day proclaimed his Turkish Cypriot Republic of Northern Cyprus in the occupied areas. With this action, he virtually partitioned the island. He also destroyed any effort at finding a lasting and viable solution to the Cyprus issue.

International reaction   International reaction to this Turkish Cypriot move was strong. It came from different directions and was considered a total contempt towards the United Nations itself, as well as of the resolutions of both the General Assembly and the Security Council. At the same time it was considered contrary to the Treaty of Guarantee of 1959, under which Britain, Greece, and Turkey, accepted the obligation to safeguard the very integrity of the Republic of Cyprus. The Security Council was the first to move. In resolution 541 of 18 November 1983, it called, among other things, on all member states not to recognise any other state in Cyprus apart from the Republic of Cyprus. The Commonwealth Congress meeting in New Delhi, also condemned the move in its own resolution on 29 Nov. 1983. The European Community also condemned the act and it even approved sanctions against the Turkish Cypriots. Despite this reaction, and encouraged by Ankara - the only capital in the world to recognize the Denktash state. Denktash stood firm as a result of this encouragement from Ankara and even threatened to colonize Varosha. Turkey also exchanged ambassadors with Denktash.

Security Council In face of these developments, the government
resolution 550 of Cyprus called for an urgent and immediate meeting of the security council which, on 11 May 1984 did issue resolution 550, considered the strongest resolution to that date on the Cyprus issue. It condemned the Turkish Cypriots as well as Turkey for the declaration of the pseudo-state and their exchange of ambassadors and asked for their immediate recall. It also called on all member states not to recognise any other government in Cyprus other than the legal government of the Republic of Cyprus. Because of the importance of this resolution, we supply it's full text. The government of Cyprus continues to insist on this resolution:

SECURITY COUNCIL RESOLUTION 550 OF 11 MAY 1984

The Security Council adopted by a vote of 13 in favour, (U.S.S.R., People Republic of China, United Kingdom, France, India, Egypt, Peru, Ukraine (S.S.R.), Upper Volta, Zaire, The Netherlands, Malta and Nicaragua) to one against (Pakistan) with one abstention (The United States of America) resolution 550 (1984) on Cyprus. The resolution reads as follows:

The Security Council,

Having considered the situation in Cyprus at the request of the government of the Republic of Cyprus,

Having heard the statement made by the President of the Republic of Cyprus,

Taking note of the report of the Secretary General (S/16519)

Recalling it's resolutions 365(1974), 367(1975), 541(1983) and 544 (1983),

Deeply regretting the non-implementation of its resolutions in particular resolution 541(1983),

Gravely concerned by the secessionist acts in the occupied part of the Republic of Cyprus which are in violation of resolution 541(1983), namely the purported "exchange of ambassadors" between Turkey and the legally invalid "Turkish Republic of Northern Cyprus" and contemplated holding of a "constitutional referendum," and "elections" as well as by other actions or threats of actions aimed at further consolidating the purported independent state and the division of Cyprus,

Deeply concerned by recent threats for settlement of Varosha by people other than its inhabitants,

Reaffirming its continuing support for the United Nations Peace-Keeping Force in Cyprus,

1. Reaffirms its resolution 541(1983) and calls for its urgent and effective implementation.

2. Condemns all secessionist actions, including the purported exchange of ambassadors between Turkey and the Turkish Cypriot leadership, declares them illegal and invalid and calls for their immediate withdrawal.

3. Reiterates the call upon all states not to recognise the purported state of the "Turkish Republic of Northern Cyprus" set up by the secessionist acts and calls upon them not to facilitate or in any way assist the aforesaid secessionist entity.

4. Calls upon all states to respect the sovereignty, independence, territorial integrity, unity and non-alignment of the Republic of Cyprus.

5. Considers attempts to settle any part of Varosha by people other than its inhabitants as inadmissible and calls for the transfer of this area to the administration of the United Nations.

6. Considers any attempts to interfere with the status or the deployment of the United Nations Peace-Keeping Force in Cyprus as contrary to the resolutions of the United Nations.

7. Requests the Secretary General to promote the urgent implementation of Security Council Resolution 541(1983).

8. Reaffirms its mandate of good offices given to the Secretary General and requests him to undertake new efforts to attain an overall solution to the Cyprus problem in confirmity with the principles of the Charter of

the United Nations and the provisions for such a settlement laid down in the pertinent United Nations resolutions, including Security Council resolution 541(1983) and the present resolution.

9. Calls upon all parties to cooperate with the Secretary General in his mission of good offices.

10. Decides to remain seized of the situation with a view to taking, in the event of non-compliance and implementation of this resolution 541 (1983) and the present resolution, urgent and appropriate measures.

11. Requests the Secretary General to promote the implementation of the present resolution and to report thereon to the Security Council as developments require.

Summit 17-20 January 1985   In his effort to break the deadlock, UN Secretary General Xavier Perez de Cuellar held three rounds of talks in New York, separately with President Kyprianou and Rauf Denktash in September, October and December. At this third round of talks Denktash appeared more conciliatory, thus giving rise to optimism. This led the Secretary General to seek a joint meeting, which was held under him in New York on 17 and 20 January 1985. The result, however, was once again negative because Denktash was not willing to have any serious discussion on matters presented, that is, the territorial the refugee, human rights, free movement, withdrawal of Turkish occupation troops, and the island's demilitarization.

New Turkish Cypriot faits accomplis   After failure of this summit meeting, Denktash proposed a new one for February which, however, never took place since Denktash and Ankara had different plans. Ignoring all Security Council resolutions Denktash called a constitutional Assembly which ratified a constitution for the Turkish Cypriots and for the Turkish Cypriot Republic of Northern Cyprus. He scheduled Presidential and Parliamentary elections. The Cyprus Government reacted strongly and immediately and condemnation by the entire international community was impressive.

George Vasiliou President   Things remained at a virtual standstill because of the negative stance of both Denktash and of Ankara. This left no room for efforts to solve the impasse. Mobility, however, came after 1988 when George Vassiliou was elected president. One of his strongest aspirations was, and remains, to solve the Cyprus issue. He decided to and did revive on the national council, in such a way that decisions on the national issue would be taken in cooperation will all political parties. The leaders and representatives of all political parties in the House of Representatives became the members of this national council. This arrangement also strengthened the position of the president internationally. An attempt by President Vassiliou to meet the Turkish prime minister, came to nothing. His invitation was refused. He did succeed in meeting Rauf Denktash, however, in Geneva in August of 1988 in the presence of the Secretary General. The Secretary General tried in vain to schedule a substantial summit meeting. Despite the unwillingness of Denktash to cooperate, President Vassiliou submitted to the Secretary General a detailed and precise document drafted and approved by the National Council, covering all aspects of the Cyprus issue. The document was received with great appreciation because of its serious approach and its realism in coping with all pending issues which make up the problem of Cyprus.

Internationalization   President Vassiliou also launched a strong campaign to internationalize the Cyprus issue. He inaugurated a series of personal contacts. This new crusade by President Vassiliou gained strength and momentum after the negative stand of Rauf Denktash in New York where they met on 26 February and 2 March under the Secretary General. The UN Secretary General did not have any hesitation in putting the blame on the Turkish Cypriot leader for the failure. Denktash had insistently demanded self determination for the two sides, or the "two people" as he put it, and not of the "two communities" which was the term used until that moment.

Cyprus-European Community   A systematic campaign was also launched to strengthen ties between the Republic of Cyprus and the European Community. This did greatly increase EC interest and involvement in the Cyprus issue. The EC blamed Ankara for the lack of a Cyprus solution and clearly stated it would not accept Turkey as a member of the community if the Cyprus problem was not solved first. At the same time, EC interest in establishing the fate of 1619 missing persons also mounted and kept the matter in the centre of attention of the international community. The matter, however, remains unresolved even though a special commission was formed to investigate it. In light of this interest and its desire to become an organic member of Europe, Cyprus applied for membership in the European Community on 4 July 1990. The Turkish Cypriots and Turkey reacted very strongly, but the EC Ministerial Council on 17 September 1990 resolved to forward the matter up to the EC commission for its examination. It is underlined that the matter is still pending.

Council of Europe and Colonists   From the establishment of the Republic in 1960, Cyprus has been, and remains an active member of the Council of Europe, which recognizes the only one legal government of Cyprus. Only the official delegations of the Cyprus Government are allowed and admitted to its meetings. The council has rejected some continual demands from the Turkish Cypriots for the council to accept representatives of the pseudo-state in the North. The Council has dealt with several matters related to the Cyprus problem, and in particular with the violation of human rights in Cyprus. It is this violation of human rights which has made 200 thousand people, Greek Cypriots, to be refugees in their own country, and has altered the demographic character of the island. The Northern part of the island, now under occupation, was, before the Turkish invasion, one of the purest Greek-Cypriot areas of the island. Now it has been converted by Turkey through its importation of some 75 thousand colonists from Anatolia. The report of Spanish Eurodeputy Alfinse Cuco is very clear on the matter. On instructions from the Council of Europe he did visit the island and studied the extent of this colonization. His report placed the colonists at 75 thousand. After study of the report the Council resolved that a population census should be held to establish in detail the extent of this colonization. The census, the Council ruled, should be held both in North and in the free areas of the island.

The Gulf Crisis   Iraq's invasion of Kuwait in 1991, the Security Council's firm stand and the decision to use force, in order to evict the invader, the U.S. and European mobilization to implement the UN decision, and the defeat of Saddam Hussein, did create a new world order which made it very clear that the law of the jungle was ended once and for all. The way in which the Gulf crisis ended gave new hopes to the people of Cyprus. They hoped that their problem would also find a solution in a just manner and that the solution would be found with the help of the United States and of Europe. Under this climate an unprecedented mobility was brought into being and it led to the mobilization of the international community itself, towards a Cyprus solution.

New Summit meetings   New summit meetings were scheduled at UN headquarters in New York. Secretary General Boutros Boutros Ghali scheduled meetings with President George Vassiliou and Rauf Denktash. Leaders of Greek Cypriot political parties were present at these meetings from July to August 1992. Results were very mearge after the refusal of Denktash to accept the Secretary General's map on the issue of territory, by his demands for an alternating presidency, about equal distribution of Ministries and so on. Under these circumstances the talks were adjourned, to resume once again on 26 October 1992. At the end of these talks the Secretary General issued his report and the SecuritY Council convened on 26 August and issued Resolution 774.

Last
Vasiliou-Denktash
meeting 26 Oct.
1992

The last meeting of President George Vasiliou and Rauf Denktash was held in New York in 26 October 1992. At this meeting Secretary General Boutros-Ghali insisted that his plan as well as his map should be accepted. The Turkish Cypriot leader insistently refused to do so. Following this development and the Secretary General's report the UN Security Council issued Resolution 789 which called for resumption of talks in March, 1993, hoping that a solution would be found.

Presidential
Elections 17 Feb
1993

This Vassiliou-Denktash meeting never took place, because in the presidential elections held on 10 and 17 February 1993, President Vassiliou lost. The new president elected was Glafcos Clerides Chairman of the Democratic Rally. (DE.SY) Clerides had played a very important part in the history of Cyprus both during the national liberation struggle of 1955-59, as well as after declaration of the republic in 1960 and later, as speaker of the House of representatives, as a member of the house and mainly as communal interlocutor. Under these circumstances the March meeting was put off until May 1993, while the international community as a whole undertook strong action in an effort to bring about a solution. What the outcome will be, at this moment remains unknown.

268